PRI

MW00593959

BY GEOFF BROWN

Copyright © 1995 Omnibus Press (A Division of Book Sales Limited)

Edited by Chris Charlesworth
Cover & Book designed by 4i
Picture research by Nikki Russell

ISBN: 0.7119.4979.4
Order No: OP 47773

Exclusive Distributors
Book Sales Limited, 8/9 Frith Street, London W1V 5TZ, UK.
Music Sales Corporation, 257 Park Avenue South, New York, NY 10010, USA.
Music Sales Pty Limited, 120 Rothschild Avenue, Rosebery, NSW 2018, Australia.

To the Music Trade only:
Music Sales Limited, 8/9 Frith Street, London W1V 5TZ, UK.

Photo credits:
All photos courtesy of LFI and Barry Plummer.
Every effort has been made to trace the copyright holders of the photographs in this book but one or two were unreachable. We would be grateful if the photographers concerned would contact us.
A catalogue record for this book is available from the British Library.

OMNIBUS PRESS
LONDON · NEW YORK · SYDNEY

CONTENTS

INTRODUCTION

If he gets his wish – and which Prince doesn't? – 1995 will see the release of 'The Golden Experience', the Paisley Park pasha's 17th album in 17 years, which as of March, 1995, Warner Bros was refusing to release. That's why his ex-Purpleness, the Artiste Formerly Known As Prince, had taken to etching SLAVE on his face prior to all photo opportunities. He is also similarly daubed while recording but as he has vowed to stay out on the road until his contractual differences with Warners are smoothed, he might not see the inside of a recording studio for some while. 'Fat chance!' I hear you cry, and rightly so. Take an estimated 500 unreleased tracks, add writing, producing and performing for a generous roster of acts, touring exhaustively and starring in three feature films and you have the profile of a man with a very serious addiction to work. It is, apparently, untreatable.

Of course, it is not essential to own all of these albums to live a full life. But two stand as the best of their decade and to track through the 15 albums and one hits collection so far released is to chart the development of a fascinating, instinctive, imaginative, idiosyncratic and productive musical talent. He has devoured and understood influences with such a thorough intelligence as to produce fresh compounds of soul, R&B, funk, pop, rock, rap and gospel with jazz grace notes. In the late Seventies his lyrics were shockingly frank about the pursuit and enjoyment of sex.

In the unshockable early Nineties, he is still singing about love and sex but God and spirituality are given space in the same hot breath. He's never been as convincing a protester or sociopolitical commentator as he has been a sexual self-publicist.

His ludicrous productivity – not a whiff of lasting artistic burn-out or concern about market saturation here – is a key component in a personality driven by fierce, single-minded ambition and the taste for competition which that frequently brings. This drive comes from a less than stable childhood which demanded

responsibility of him early on. He's small, physically slight and endured a fair amount of frustration and bullying because of it. Excellence is a fine way to hit back at this cheap sort of ridicule and from the cares and woe he escaped into music. His grasp of musical styles, often quite staggering in its breadth, and of musical instruments and recording techniques, gave him the weapons he needed. He never grew physically big but he grew good-looking in an androgynous handsome/pretty way and, early on, sang some of the most profane pre-rap lyrics in a falsetto voice that entirely lacked threat. His best music has nearly always kept closest to African American roots though he can rock'n'roll with the best. None of his peers organises bands so well.

A thumbnail sketch of his early years reads: Born Minneapolis, 7 June, 1958, to Mattie and John L Nelson, a piano player. Parents divorced when he was seven, both remarried. At 14, moved in with best friend André Anderson (later named Cymone) and Bernadette Anderson's five other children. A couple of years later, he and André formed

Grand Central. In the early Seventies, the Minneapolis music scene was remote and local radio stations were unimaginative. Like all bands, they started by playing cover versions but the distance from mainstream American music encouraged creativity. It also gave a taste for listening to and relying on internal, not external voices.

Grand Central became Champagne who cut a record at Chris Moon's studio in Minneapolis. Prince was 17. He left the group and started working with Moon, writing two of the songs which would appear two years later on his 1978 solo début. After an unsuccessful trip to New York to get a major label deal, hometown businessman Owen Husney took Prince on. He recorded more demos and tracks with Pepe Willie's band 94 East, which later surfaced as 'Minneapolis Genius – The Historic 1977 Recordings'. Eventually, Husney got him an unprecedented self-production deal with Warner Bros after top producers Gary Katz, Russ Titelman and Ted Templemann and A&R chief Lenny Waronker had 'auditioned' him.

He created a wild, exotic and precocious image from the start by dropping two names (Roger Nelson), two years (born 1960 according to his early Press releases), and two hundred hints about his promiscuity, none of which seemed a big deal in showbiz terms.

But the way he wrote about sex *was* headline news. A painfully shy interviewee, as I discovered to my bewilderment in 1981, he soon broke off 'normal' contact with the media. At first, this increased his mystique. Later, it turned into open season on ridicule which has focused attention away from his music, the one thing he does well, if not too wisely some of the time.

After innumerable Purple puns, he invited the world to address him as a hieroglyph, a preposterous notion inviting further remorseless derision. He has become a Godsend to any columnist desperate for that last whimsical paragraph. But whatever he is called, he ought to be judged by his extraordinarily prolific musical output. This is it.

FOR YOU

(FIRST RELEASE – APRIL 1978 ON WARNER BROS BSK 3150; US CD 3150-2.
UK: VINYL WEA K 56989, CD K 2-56989)

Prince signed his contract with Warner Bros in June, 1977, a couple of weeks after his 19th birthday. He was still claiming to be a couple of years younger. Before signing, he'd been 'auditioned' by a trio of the company's trusted producers because the deal allowed him unusual privileges – playing all of the instruments, arranging and producing the material – and clearly they were a little sceptical of his all-round ability and had a financial investment to protect.

After rejecting a list of potential producers and finding others, like Earth, Wind & Fire's Maurice White, busy elsewhere, Warners relented and allowed Prince to produce his own tracks. But they insisted that an experienced engineer, Tommy Vicari, supervise and advise at the desk as 'executive producer'.

When I interviewed Prince in 1981, he didn't say much about anything at all but he was fairly dismissive, in a monosyllabic, sighing sort of way, of Vicari's input. The writer/singer/musician gleaned some engineering skills.

Recorded at the Record Plant in Sausalito, California, the album took five months to make, and was released on 7 April, 1978. It sold no more than respectably – about 150,000 – and made 163 on the *Billboard* chart. The first single, 'Soft And Wet'/'So Blue' was released on his 20th birthday (his 18th according to early Press biographies).

Although he was promoted to the world at large as a teenage prodigy with an extravagant and mature talent, his first fans were teenagers, kids not much younger than himself. He received a lot of attention and exposure in teen magazines. The album's sleeve, with its back-lit photograph of the Afro-ed star, was probably intended to engender a sense of mystery, his hypnotic stare suggesting someone who can gaze deep into your soul. But, quality of the eyes aside, the sleeve actually looks merely rather plain and uninteresting. The inner sleeve, with head-on and left and right profile shots of Prince, sitting on a satin quilted bed, naked with a strategically placed guitar in his lap, is rather more in keeping with the man to come.

The 'For You' album is a satisfactory if a touch lightweight introduction to his raw talent. Almost without exception these are love songs, though already he shows a propensity to take a rather more singular spin on love than is customarily heard in the pop charts. But so keen is he to show us what he can do in a variety of styles – black pop music and funk occasionally lightly spiced by the use of jazz harmonies or the lilt and sway of reggae, and, of course, rock – that there's no sense of the solid direction and the full, thought-out agenda that would become the hallmark of his best albums in the Eighties and Nineties.

And the album sleeve leaves us in no doubt that the young Minneapolitan is the virtual sole creator of the music. The 'Produced, Arranged, Composed and Performed by Prince' credits dominate his first five recordings to this day. On vinyl, he split the album as 'Side One' and 'The Other Side'.

For You

Barely more than five seconds long, Prince introduces us to his distinctive voice in a brief, lush, multi-layered prayer-like *a capella* piece. In the course of his first four albums he will sing, almost exclusively, in falsetto. This actually makes it easier for other singers to cover his songs because when they sing in their 'normal' range they have a better chance of making the lyric and melody their own. Compare Meli'sa Morgan's 'Do Me Baby' or Chaka Khan's 'I Feel For You' to the original and see how easy his falsetto has made it for them to reinterpret the song.

In Love

A cute pop strut, not unlike the style developed by Brothers Johnson under the aegis of Quincy Jones, grounded by a good 4/4 funk bass throb. He creates the track with a battery of keyboard hardware and guitars – Orr bass, Ms. Poly Moog, syndrums, Arp Pro Soloist, Arp String Ensemble and syndrums. He sings in falsetto and the gift for libidinous imagery is immediately obvious in lines such as 'I really wanna play in your river'. Lifejackets will be worn hereafter. For an opening statement, the pop appeal of 'In Love' is plenty self-evident. It was the B-side of his second single, 'Just As Long As We're Together'.

Soft And Wet

Like 'In Love' but more so in every department. The cute pop button is pressed harder, the slightly faster 4/4 rhythm with its jerkier arrangement engages more with the dance-floor, and the lyrics take more risks. Like much of his uptempo material at this time, 'Soft And Wet's' mixture of light pop appeal and driving funk has much in common with the better work of Graham Central Station, the band formed by former Sly Stone bassist Larry Graham a few years earlier. Although the lyric does not seem quite so audacious in the Nineties of bragging gangsta rap, in the *pop* charts of the late Seventies there was not a lot of this sort of writing done. Donna Summer's heavy breathing disco hits had prepared the ground; Prince's gasps and susspurations are, in retrospect, a trial run for more graphic moaning to, er, come, as it were. But this was certainly quite hot stuff from an act that was initially marketed fairly exclusively at the teen audience through, Warners hoped, a good share of airplay. Nonetheless, in the US the single 'Soft And Wet' sold 350,000, reached 12 on the black charts and 92 pop.

Crazy You

Prince temporarily decommissioned his Synthesizer Armoured Division for this acoustic sound. A relaxed guitar intro establishes a simple, attractive figure followed by melody to match. He uses finger cymbals, wind chimes, congas and water drums to create an atmosphere that catches the mood of lyrics describing a 'so strung out' state of mind.

Just As Long As We're Together

The second single, released in November, 1978. After the simplicity of 'Crazy You', 'Just As Long' is an upbeat song with a real spring in its step, again reminiscent in feel of the uptempo material of Graham Central Station. This is more noticeable because for once he decides against using falsetto vocals throughout. The fade comprises a long funk vamp – it could have been wilder – but his bass develops the sort of drive which became familiar on his later albums. The single flopped reaching 91 on the black charts.

Baby

First track on 'The Other Side' of the vinyl release, 'Baby' presents the tangible results of the soft and wet passions described on side one. The 'baby' of the title is indeed an infant. He never thought that this would happen to a 'careful' man like him, he sings to a slow arrangement. In pop music, 'baby' has traditionally meant lover and to hear it used so literally is refreshing. After layered vocals and decorative doo-wopping, the song about unexpected pregnancy is resolved with the hope that their child 'has eyes just like yours'.

My Love Is Forever

An introduction to his feel for and grasp of vocal group technique, although all the multi-tracked voices are his own. The track has a good, jaunty, uptempo feel and drive and he flexes his guitar with a solo and some nice phrasing.

So Blue

The B-side of 'Soft And Wet' is a falsetto ballad which kicks off with a nimble bass figure and acoustic guitar chording. It's a song about loss and although Prince had already experienced his fair share of it, the track lacks weight.

I'm Yours

In which Prince gets his rocks off. After a funk bass intro, he straps on an electric guitar and gets down in a serious rock band context. The guitar riff, and much of the track, feels and sounds at odds with the rest of the album. In fact the middle eight, with its quite catchy pop melody, sounds at odds with the rest of the track. The whole has a strange, stitched together quality. The track exits, guitar riffing wildly.

PRINCE

(FIRST RELEASE IN US , OCTOBER 1979 ON WARNER BROS BSK 3366, CD 3366-2. UK VINYL K 56772)

After a brief promotional tour, Prince put together a band to take the music on the road. Like Sly Stone a decade earlier, the group he put together was multi-racial and mixed sex. This was still an extremely rare set-up despite the success of Sly &The Family Stone and the passing of ten 'enlightened' years. One of the reasons he gave at the time was that too many of his African-American musician friends listened to too narrow a range of music.

Prince's close friend André Andersen, renamed Cymone, came in on bass; the white drummer Bobby Rivkin, who had worked on Prince's demo tape, was now known as Bobby Z and completed the rhythm section. Rivkin was David's brother and had played with Pepe Willie's 94 East. Lead guitarist Dez Dickerson from St Paul had played in some local bands, and the two white keyboard players, who got the job ahead of Jimmy Jam Harris, were Matt Fink and Gayle Chapman, the first of many women musicians Prince would employ.

The Minneapolis minstrel had been underwhelmed by the sales of his début album, for which he blamed inadequate promotion. One of the solutions he came up with was to quit Owen Husney's American Artists. A degree of pain and rancour was involved. Soon after came Prince's début concerts as a solo name on January 5 and 6, 1979, at the Capri Theatre, Minneapolis, one show for Joe Public, one for Warner Bros wheels keen for a glimpse of their investment. All parties felt that there was a lot of promise but this was not yet the finished article. He signed for management with Hollywood heavyweights (Bob) Cavallo, (Joe) Ruffalo and (Steve) Fargnoli in the summer of 1979. Over time, Fargnoli was the firm's partner who had most involvement with Prince's career.

Another remedy for what he felt were the poor sales of 'For You' was a brisker rate of recording. Having laboured for five months on his first album, the second one took him six weeks. He used Alpha Studios in Burbank, California and again produced, arranged, composed and performed all nine tracks. This time, there was no label-nominated and appointed 'executive producer' to keep a beady eye on things and offer advice where it seemed prudent or useful to do so.

A third course of action was, simply and pragmatically, to record more overtly commercial songs. Later for art and messages. What's the point of making grand statements if no-one's listening? Before we get serious, we get known. In general, the vocals on 'Prince' are less layered and his playing is sharper and more confident.

Of his band, only André Cymone and Bobby Z are credited on the album sleeve as 'Heaven-sent helpers'. The others get a mention on the inner sleeve. The cure worked, as 'Prince' gave him his first American Top 20 single and his first No 1 on the black singles charts. By April 1980, the album itself had sold over 500,000, qualifying for Gold, and went on to sell a million.

The packaging of the album was certainly simpler. A head-and-shoulders shot of an apparently naked Prince against a pale blue background with his name, scripted in dark pink, hovering above him like a halo. The dot over the 'i' is replaced by a heart. The stare this time is less hypnotic, blanker, as though hypnotised by the camera. The lips seem slightly pursed. On the back sleeve he's pictured perched on a white winged horse, a messenger arriving on Pegasus with all the hot news from the gods.

This time we can actually read the news on the inner sleeve. Prince seems to take an *ad hoc* attitude to making his lyrics more easily accessible to the listener. Sometimes there's a sheet, sometimes not. The portrait on the inner-sleeve is again Prince's head and upper torso. This time he's wearing a leather jacket, wildly over-dressed for him really. The inner sleeve makes no specific mention of the array of keyboard hardware used on the tracks.

I Wanna Be Your Lover

Released in the States two months before the album on 24 August, 1979, 'I Wanna Be' was the big pop breakthrough mentioned above, capitalising on the teen buzz created by 'Soft And Wet', appealing to the white pop and black markets and creating a ripple on late Seventies dancefloors. It's a very simple and catchy song and is an early signpost to what will later be called the Minneapolis sound.

Driven from the opening by chopped guitar chords on all four beats of the 4/4 bars – and which recur with every chorus – the song presents the plea of a po' boy and a shy boy who is trying to win back his girl. The minx has been temporarily seduced by the blandishments of the better-off cats she hangs out with. But his love, once awakened, will be an altogether more encompassing beast. He wants to be her lover, brother, mother, sister. Hey, here's monogamy – he wants to be the only one she comes for! It was, in fact, written for the multi-instrumentalist/singer Patrice Rushen, on whom he had a crush, but she wasn't interested. In the song Prince's falsetto vocal suggests both the vulnerable naïvety of adolescent love and its supreme confidence given half-a-gram of encouragement. Speaking of encouragement, the single sold a million. It was released as a single in the UK in December. Millie Jackson covered the song in 1987.

Why You Wanna Treat Me So Bad

An early example of his use of powerful, melodic rock guitar, the track was released as the second single off the album in January, 1980. Big flop. Which is strange because lyric-wise he's still having big problems with the girlfriend. It's the second song on this album that he originally wrote for Patrice Rushen. The rocker – phrases, licks, arrangement, solo – turned off black radio, which had championed 'I Wanna Be Your Lover', and the African-American teenagers, predominantly, who'd bought it. The times were perhaps less ready for such a mixing of black and white styles on one album. In the Nineties, of course, you're a sucker if you don't mix rap and rock.

Sexy Dancer

A blueprint for many of Prince's sweaty, butt-bumpin', groin-humpin' dancefloor shakin' tracks. If you are looking for a minimalist lyric, end your search right now. Take the words 'sexy' and 'dancer' add the phrase 'I want your body', rearrange in as many ways as possible and pant heavily and often. It's an effective cut, though, because he organises the instru-

mental funk track so well. Cue bass, chicken-scratch guitar, vocals, then add organ. It's a funk and dance breeze.

When We're dancing Close And Slow

Prince took a while to become as comfortable with slow songs as he is with uptempo pieces. This slowie is not a success. There's a Japanese feel to the chord changes as he virtually talks his way through the lyric. In fact, the words intrude on the mood created by his music. But the lyric does have an early example of the way he uses the proximity of mouth and brain to suggest the closeness of senses and the mind. When they kiss hard, he tells his girl, he can almost taste her thoughts. Sex as mind control?

With You

Continuing the slow dancing mood of 'When We're Dancing', 'With You' is just as unsuc-cessful. The lyric is a rather touching admis-sion of constancy in love, of fear of losing a true lover. Sadly, the falsetto does not con-vince on this occasion.

Bambi

Dominated by guitar, this hard rock plod is hewn from a similar piece of stone as 'Why You Wanna Treat Me So Bad?' It contains one of his more notorious early couplets. Picture it. He's fallen for the girl Bambi but, life's frustrations being what they are, she turns out to be a lesbian. 'Bambi, it's better with a man,' he sings, rather shrilly. This scenario was still not much discussed within the lyrics of pop music in 1979 and it must be admitted that his response is less than PC. All red-bloodied American male, in fact, as he drags 'Bambi' off to be shown what it's like to be loved by a man.

Still Waiting

For love, not a Number 9 bus. Here is sweet simplicity. He's waiting for a first real love and conveys a genuine sense of longing, not too desperate at first, but palpable and growing. It's a simple tune and he sings it very, well, *nicely*. Many girls, hearing this and gazing at the serious face gazing back at them from the album sleeve, will have decided to make him wait no longer.

I Feel For You

Like the songs on the first album, much of the material Prince prepared for the second album came from ideas he'd worked on before he put his name to the Warners contract. This is by far the most impressive of them. And not only because it was a big hit for Chaka Khan. It's a great, feelgood pop song. From the opening organ figure, this is happy, happy dance music and it must remain something of a mystery as to why this was never released as a single. Major error.

It's Gonna Be Lonely

A final ballad. This is a fine example of what it is to be young, in love and insecure. You get to thinking what it would be like if *your* girlfriend/boyfriend left. You talk to her/him about it, worry about it, talk to her/him about it some more and then you find you've talked her/him into leaving.

DIRTY MIND

(FIRST US RELEASE, OCTOBER, 1980 WARNER BROS BSK 3478, CD 3478-2.

UK VINYL WEA K 56862, CD K 2-56862)

❝Love and lust in Minneapolis' read the *Rolling Stone* headline. 'A pop record of Rabelaisian achievement' wrote its reviewer, who went on to marvel at Prince's talent. 'Just barely twenty, he's written, produced and played all the instruments on each of his three LPs.' The lie Owen Husney suggested about his age had taken root – Prince was approaching his 23rd birthday – but that does not diminish the scope of his achievement. For 'Dirty Mind' was the album that turned Prince from black pop prodigy into something far more potent, even though its initial sale was only half that of 'Prince'.

The approach to funk and rock were harder, the lighter pop appeal of the first two albums remains but is secondary to the more adult nature of the content. Prince the devoted lover has become a love man who knows dark secrets. He is running uptown and downtown in something less than his night gown - so are all the ladies in their beds because Prince is coming round. Of course there was a big danger inherent in this shift into more adult material. He stood to lose the young teen audience which had helped to make 'I Wanna Be Your Lover' a No 1. It does not take much of an imagination to picture what might happen in God-fearing homes when a young son or daughter of less than voting age brought home their very own 'Dirty Mind'.

Never mind the music, the album sleeve set the tone. Dressed only in black briefs, a scarf and a raincoat with a studded right shoulder and, pinned to the left lapel, a badge bearing the legend 'Rude Boy', Prince is apparently laying on bed springs. No mattress, just bed springs. His hair is shorter, tidier. On the back sleeve, he's reclining on something softer, same togs but we can see his legs. He's wearing thick black stockings and boots. Sprayed grafitti on the wall behind him are the titles of the songs on the album. Minneapolis seemed like a weird place, not at all what one would expect of a mid-West state like Minnesota.

And then there was the band. Snapped for

the inner sleeve. Bobby Z in suit and tie, André
Andersen and Dez Dickerson in raincoats and
neckwear, no shirt or jacket. The zip of
Andre's jeans is half undone. Dez wears loud,
checkerboard patterned trousers. Lisa
Coleman, who replaced Gayle Chapman on
keyboards in the summer of 1980 and will also
gasp effectively on several tracks while she is
with the band, wears a thin, belted mac. Dr
(Matt) Fink, keyboard player, is dressed as a
surgeon. One who wears shades. Would
he play keyboards with those surgeon's
gloves on?

This imagery evolved through the spring
American tour as support act to Rick James,
during which a vitriol-fuelled rivalry between
the two was fanned. James had dubbed his
music punk-funk. Prince was as much puckish
as punk. But his band's evolving look usurped
the streetsy look that James, a more traditional soul act, never wholly embraced.

None of this, however, quite prepared the
listener for the nine tracks Prince selected for
'Dirty Mind'. 'My lyrics are everyday talk that
goes on around me all the time,' he said. 'It's
basically about my life and the different

things I've experienced,' he later added. Here was an examination of the contemporary sexual mores of the boys and girls which would confirm the worst fears of any parent. The album was recorded in Minneapolis – engineered by Jamie Starr, the first pseudonym Prince used on his albums – and he again produced, arranged, composed and performed everything apart from Dr Fink's co-writing credit on the title track.

No surprise that Warner Bros, too, were a touch nonplussed by the album. Expecting to start the Eighties with a consolidating pop follow-up to a pop million-seller, they got a guy wearing some of his sister's clothes singing about sex in many permutations and places and in ever-increasing graphic detail. But confrontation is the point of the album. 'Dirty Mind' faces down preconceptions of every type. OK, mostly sexual. There is wry humour, there is libidinous romping, there is political pronouncement, there is straight talking. With some misgivings, Warners released the record with most of the tracks only minimally altered from the original Minneapolis-recorded demos. ('Recorded somewhere in Uptown'

the inner sleeve cryptically notes.)

It sold less well than 'Prince' despite the *Rolling Stone* review, which gave 'Dirty Mind' four-and-a-half stars out of five and followed with a live review and interview under the headline 'Will the little girls understand'. If they did, they weren't letting on. Bottom line – Prince had been in step with the pop and dance audience. Now he was trying to tap into a wider market. He wasn't in step any more. 'Dirty Mind' was several paces in front. Not all reviewers acclaimed the album. In *Billboard*, Nelson George thought the lyrics 'overt examples of quite disgusting immaturity'.

Of course, it helped that some of the situations about which he writes and sings on 'Dirty Mind' are taken from his own life though he did not specify which when I talked to him in 1981. But then he did not specify much at all back then. Although he had not yet become an entire hermit when faced with media interest, he was a profoundly unenthusiastic interviewee, not hostile but shut as tight as a sea anemone at low tide. Warners must have heavied him into giving the few interviews he managed to sit through on that first tour. I still have one of the company's UK press releases from that time and it shows how well he was known, even by his own company, on this side of the Atlantic. 'Dirty Mind' was apparently his second, not third, album ('For You' did not exist). The members of his band were listed: Andre Samone, Dex Dickerson, Bobby Lee and Gail Chapman were spelt incorrectly – and Chapman had quit anyhow – but they got Matt Fink's name right.

Dirty Mind

There is much to admire in the lack of ambiguity of albums that start the way they mean to go on. This is one of them. The track starts with a bass throb and thudding 4/4 rhythm The drive and momentum is harder. Although the instrumentation is much the same as on 'Prince' and there's certainly not the piled-high vocal overlays of 'For You', the sound is fuller, deeper, and hits the dancefloor hard. Instruments ebb and flow in and out of the mix but the constant pulse of the 4/4 is paramount as Prince sings the praises of sex in cars, sex under the stars, sex anywhere in fact. And if you find these recreational, procreational bodi

ly functions 'dirty', it's all the fault of his luscious and tempting girlfriend who zaps the synapses of his mind. The track was released as a US single, the second off the album, in November, 1980.

When You Were Mine

There was something on the album for the pop fans after all. Virtually a throwback in style to the beat groups of the sixtiès, 'Mine' recalls Beatles harmonies and the simplicity, energy, effectiveness, and vivacity of the basic guitar-bass-drums group line-up. The lyrics reveal a happy-sounding guy willing to put up with any amount of off-hand treatment from his girlfriend. She took his money, wore his clothes, brought other men to his bed. But now she's gone, he loves her more.

Do It All Night

Good funk with a superior bass line, some very fine soul shouting and a rigorous instrumental vamp. The latter is probably one result of his tour. Although as a support act he would get little chance to stretch out, time being limited, rehearsing with a band opens up the possibilities of the band jam. On record, of course, where he played all of the instruments himself, maintaining the spontaneity inherent in a vamp at the end of a tune is not particularly easy after the fourth overdub. Superfluous to explain what it is they're doing all night, isn't it?

Gotta Broken Heart Again

The album's only ballad, 'Broken Heart' is actually taken at a quicker lick than most 'ballads' (these days ballad seems to mean slow song, which is not always the case). He's in falsetto range and the 'clang' at the end of the track slams like a cell door closing on his latest affair.

Uptown

Party time! The first single off the album released in the US in September, 1980. This is one of Prince's first attempts to put his view of the perfect society into a song. In lyrics, he pictures it as free from prejudice – racial, sexual, social – and musically he hears it as a fast, fun, get down funky place to be. The African-American audience agreed. Although it failed to make the pop charts, 'Uptown' was a Top 5

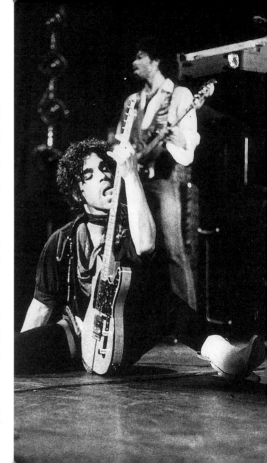

single on the black charts. 'Uptown' is also one of the songs which bassist André Cymone felt he'd had a hand in composing and which hastened his disgruntled departure. 'Uptown' segues into. . .

Head

One of two songs which, even more than the title tune, snapped listeners to attention. Did they hear that lyric right? They did. It is an outrageously self-confident if improbable tale. He meets a virgin bride en route to the altar, tries out his seduction technique and, briefly enflamed, they indulge in audibly gratifying oral sex. The music's tight and spare with a poppin' funk bass and synthesiser motif driving the track. Prince credits help – Matt Fink as co-composer (maybe it happened to *him!!)* and man at the synthesiser, and Lisa Coleman as vocalist, though much of this is sighing and panting. (Maybe it happened to *her!!* – the song had been too much for Gayle Chapman, who left soon after it was introduced into the repertoire.) It segues into. . .

Sister

The second of the two tunes which demanded careful listening. In a brief, frantic pop-funk blast, the narrator admits bisexuality and incest. Wilfully contentious, it presses the right buttons to get the full attention of any self-respecting critic. Sequenced right after 'Head', it was impossible to ignore the challenging, shocking nature of these tracks, willing you to be censorious. Or to come along for the ride. It segued into. . .

Partyup

A driving, good-time album closer. The funk fizzes along and the lyrics turn into a series of chants about not giving a damn, they just want to jam and warning the Government to fight its own wars, because they wouldn't. 'There were a few anti-draft demonstrations going on that I was involved in that spurred me to write 'Partyup',' Prince once said. Which is contradicted somewhat by the recollections of both Dez Dickerson and Minneapolis singer Alexander O'Neal. They have alleged that 'Partyup' was heavily based on a song written by The Time's Morris Day. In return for Prince's assistance in getting The Time a recording contract with Warner Bros, Day gave the song to Prince who altered it a little and called it his own. Whatever, it ends an album that announced Prince as an artist with an agenda.

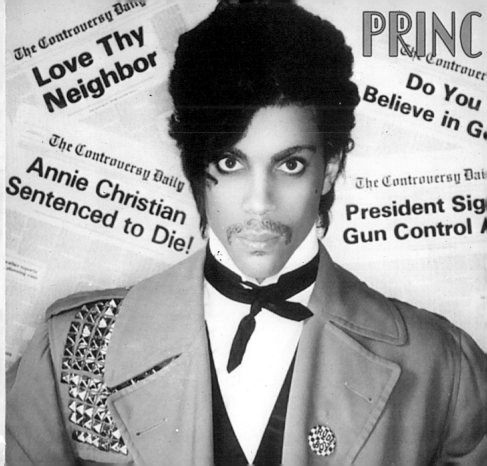

CONTROVERSY

(ORIGINAL RELEASE, OCTOBER, 1981 US WARNER BROS BSK 3601, CD 3601-2.
UK: WEA K 56950, CD K 2-56950.)

The fourth Prince album and second in the sequence of adult-oriented funk – adult-oriented in terms of lyric content, not the geriatric connotations of AOR – which characterised his extraordinarily productive spell at the start of the Eighties. Concurrently with writing and recording 'Dirty Mind', and with touring and writing and recording 'Controversy', he had also written and co-produced the début album by The Time (under the name Jamie Starr). He has been locked in Rampantly Prolific Mode ever since.

It does not take a huge leap of the imagination to grasp the fact that a proportion of 'Controversy' is autobiographical. Although 'Dirty Mind' did not sell as well as its predecessor, its controversial content certainly drew the column inches. Not for the last time, Prince had been in papers more, and for longer, than he was in the charts. The new album's sleeve suggested as much. The front and back illustrations comprise a random scattering of front page headlines from 'The Controversial Daily'. The headlines – 'Tourist Invasion of Uptown Fails, 89 Beheaded!' 'The Second Coming', 'President Signs Gun Control Act', 'Love Thy Neighbour', 'Annie Christian Sentenced To Die', 'Do You Believe In God', 'Joni' [Mitchell, a great favourite] –

mix the screams of sensationalism with spiritual messages. Already the pull between the profane and the sacred is surfacing in his work. And Prince kept his clothes on for the album sleeve snap.

Sexual politics and sexual narratives formed the core of 'Dirty Mind'. But Prince's agenda is now far wider than the merely personal. Throughout 'Controversy' the spotlight is shone less relentlessly on the libido. There's more than a hint of the wider issues to be addressed more frequently on the better of his later albums.

The title track was released as a single in September, 1981, and went to No 3 on the black charts but stalled at 70 on the pop charts. He was stuck at crossover junction.

Couldn't cross the tracks. The invitation to support The Rolling Stones in Los Angeles a week before the albums' American release seemed heaven sent.

Alas, the sentiment was not mutual as far as The Rolling Stones' audience was concerned. Used as a sounding board for insults, Prince fled the stage after 20 minutes of the first night and returned to Minneapolis. Persuaded to return for the second night, Prince met an audience better prepared. He and the band were pelted with a barrage of objects and fled after three numbers. For a man preparing to sing of freedom, tolerance and understanding this must have been a salutary experience of the lack of these qualities in a blinkered rock audience.

The fourth album was again recorded in Minneapolis (aka Uptown) and with the production, arranging, performing and writing all credited to Prince, apart from Lisa Coleman's backing vocals on three tracks and Bobby Z's drumming and Lisa and Matt Fink's keyboard playing on one track. The music – performance and arrangement – is even sparer than on 'Dirty Mind'. And, importantly, Prince limits

his use of falsetto vocals. The best tracks are impressively tight as this album, and 'The Time' set, bring the Minneapolis sound as evolved in Prince's kingdom to the brink of maturity. The American tour to promote 'Controversy', with

The Time supporting, was a big success and helped to push the album up the US charts to a high of 21. His reputation as one of the best live performers of his generation has never been challenged with any consistency. Certainly, some shows are better than others but the standards he has set himself as a live act are much higher than those set by almost all of his contemporaries.

Controversy

As noted above, the album's first single. This is not the seed of the Minneapolis Sound, this is the full grown plant. The bass throb gets lift and bounce from both the hard 4/4 beat and the delicate chicken-scratch guitar chording in the mix. There is a wash of synthesiser sound. The cut chugs. It's prime pop-funk. The lyric is a pretty obvious comment on his life in the media over the preceding couple of years. Clearly, he did not expect the level of media attention his lyrics and act were attracting, which seems a tad naïve. The questions about his religious beliefs and sexual orientation, among others, were the spur. He recites the Lord's Prayer and in a kind of schoolyard chant sets out a few wishes of his own: that there was no black or white and no rules.

Sexuality

Well, you might think, the title's a bit of a give away. In fact sex is only one of the many topics addressed in this headlong charge of a manifesto. He's got so many Big Things to say and he needs to say them fast. The jungle thrum of a tom-tom and a strange, squealing shout lead into a relentless track that *sounds* pretty macho. He urges a new breed of leaders – 'stand up, organise' – encourages revolution, a world without segregation, the freedom of mind and body. What's preventing this, he sings, are among other things the generations of illiterate children conditioned by TV. Educate them and there is hope for all.

Do Me, Baby

A terrific ballad. Sung falsetto, keyboards, drums and a poppin' bass provide the springboard to one of Prince's subtler seduction scenes that makes the very windows steam up. Beyond that, there is not a lot to be said about it other than that she finally does it to him half way through the track and great are the acrobatic ecstatics. Sometimes, he observes, he likes to sit down and watch. 'Do Me' is another song which, it is alleged, was written by André Andersen and later adopted as his own by Prince. A version was allegedly recorded in New York at the same time as the tracks which formed the 'Minneapolis Genius' album. 'Do Me' also became the sensuous title track of Meli'sa Morgan's 1986 album.

Private Joy

On vinyl, this pop song started the second side of the album. After the deep satisfaction of the first three tracks, particularly 'Do Me, Baby' and the title track, this was fluff. It's a jerky, jaunty piece with layered harmonies upon which Prince relies in his less substantial pop songs, 'Private Joy' is lyrically obtuse in that he could be singing about a woman, a sexual aid, masturbation or all three. The arrangement bolsters the song with a bass solo, a guitar solo which is based on feedback and a passage in which 16s beat on a tom-tom like the sound of blood pounding in the brain.

The rat-a-tat-tat of machine gun fire segues the track into...

Ronnie, Talk To Russia

Our ambassador from Minneapolis advises Mr Reagan to negotiate before the world is blown to bits. As a clear-eyed analysis of the global situation, this was a laughable piece of political polemic. Real panic is suggested by the manic, punk pace of the track and the hard rock/metal guitar solos.

Let's Work

Straightforward and enjoyably tight Minneapolis funk with considerable dance appeal. Load-bearing bass and synthesisers carry the track. There is sweaty comparison between work on the dancefloor and work in bed. It segues via a drum machine into...

Annie Christian

More controversy. Most of the newspaper headlines on the album's cover find an echo on the record. Prince underlines the newsworthiness of the highly-publicised murders and attempted murders listed here by speaking the lyrics in the sober tone of a TV newscaster. Gun control is one of the recurring debates in the USA and with the right to bear arms enshrined in the Constitution is likely to remain so for some years to come. In part, 'Annie Christian' can be seen as Prince's contribution to the debate. He's agin 'em.

As witnesses for his prosecution he produces the murder of John Lennon, the assassination attempt on Ronald Reagan and the murders of black children in Atlanta. He goes further by trying to identify the devil in the heart or mind or soul of the perpetrators. It was one who wanted to be No 1 but whose kingdom never came – i.e. the angel who fell from grace, Satan – who is identified in the deconstructed language of streetspeak. 'Annie Christian' = anti-Christian. It's a mean and puzzling society into which people no longer fit and values are warped. Some, maybe many, people find it difficult to make a niche in this hard world. And when they lash out, the media, to return to the theme of 'Controversy', is only too willing to give that niche. For a while. It's a recurring theme most recently treated by Oliver Stone's *Natural Born Killers*.

Jack U Off

Lest all of this get a bit too heavy, Prince closes by running down for us the convenience and pleasure of mutual masturbation in public places. Cinema, restaurant, wherever. And, a rare thing, he called Lisa, Bobby Z and Matt Fink in to the studio to play on the track. It's here too that his use of symbols begins with single letters standing in for whole words in song titles. You becomes U.

1999

(FIRST RELEASE OCTOBER, 1982 US VINYL WARNER BROS 23720-1, CD 2-23720.
UK WEA 923720-1, CD WEA 923720-2)

In a quite astounding burst of productivity, Prince recorded his best album to date, drawing a line under the development of his style through the black pop of the first two albums and the darker, sexier, funkier, lewder, more varied, more adventurous and riskier songs on 'Dirty Mind' and 'Controversy'. '1999' ushered him into the big time as he crossed over into the white rock market.

The Controversy tour had been a snowballing success as his ability to outrage transferred seamlessly from record to stage. Whether he was disrobing – getting the kit off has become commonplace but his strips were notable for their lascivious tease to please the young girls – or simulating crucifixion, here was a show aimed at broadening the audience appeal. The publicity he was attracting was bound to excite the interest of rock fans who'd not heard a note of his music.

Back home in Minneapolis, his basement studio had been upgraded to accommodate a 24-track facility and he embarked on a period of high output, one of several of which have peppered his career. In the early part of 1982 he put together the girl trio Vanity 6 and as Jamie Starr wrote and produced the bulk of the material on their début album, a somewhat exploitative collection of sexually-obsessed songs by women in underwear. One need say no more than that he originally intended to call the trio The Hookers. The album sold well though, No 6 on the black album charts and Top 50 pop. And as the Starr Company, he produced 'What Time Is It', The Time's second album, which reached No 2 on the black album charts. The single '777-9311' peaked at No 2 on the black chart.

By the summer he was working on his own music. 'He knew it was back to dance,' drummer Bobby Z said. No more 'Ronnie, Talk To Russia'. 'There was some weird stuff, but it was still very funky. He found his groove and the groove never left.' The sessions were so productive that he had enough for a double album, and then some. Not that the record company in England agreed, and cut it to a single album. One had some sympathy with this notion. The third and fourth sides meander compared to the tight excellence of the first two sides. The double album format seems to have persuaded him to let a couple of tracks vamp on where a swifter conclusion would have been preferable. But, over a decade later, the album remains a very strong musical statement, a testimony to Prince's abilities and energy at the time.

With its three hit singles, '1999' established him in the rock market. A new live show using the same band as on the Controversy tour hit the road in November 1982 and stayed there until mid-April, 1983 by which time the *Los Angeles Times* would be comparing its revolutionary impact to David Bowie's 'Ziggy Stardust' tour, Bruce Springsteen's 'Born To Run' dates and the Sex Pistols' 'Anarchy In The US' tour. He was named Rock Artist of the Year in the *Rolling Stone* Critics' Awards.

The set concentrated on his increasingly confident singing, playing and dancing and toned down the crasser aspects of his previous tours' sexual theatrics. There was high energy and genuine sense of fun and exuberance and less of the lewd adolescent . It could be argued that he was taking fewer chances – and by playing safe was gaining access to a much wider audience – but the basic subject matter of almost all of '1999' remains sex in its multifarious forms. But it seems indisputable that if he had continued down the overtly lewd path trod by the Dirty Mind and Controversy tours, he would have run an even greater risk of being turned in to the King Leer of pop. More simply, the live show matched the maturity of the album it was promoting.

The album went gold in the States by January, 1983 and sold over a million by the end of that year. Outside the USA, the double and single versions of the album sold a million, by far his biggest international success up to that date, and the title track was his first UK chart single. Not for the last time, he cancelled a one-off UK date.

Cold feet in the UK led WEA to put out a single LP version of '1999' omitting 'D.M.S.R.', 'Automatic', 'All The Critics Love U In New York' and 'International Lover'.

1999

The title track is the glorious summation of Princely pop-funk. It opens with a crash of drum machinery and a simple four-note synthesiser phrase which anchors the melody. The drum machine lays down the irresistible 4/4 dance rhythm. 'Don't worry' he slurs from a slowed tape. 'I won't hurt you. I only want to have some fun.' The vocals are shared between Prince, Lisa Coleman and Dez Dickerson singing a line a piece throughout the verses.

The effect of this constant changing of vocal tone – from Coleman's higher, cleaner voice to Dickerson's deeper, rougher textured sound and Prince's, pitched midway between the two – was heightened by the circumstances of its recording. According to Alan Leeds, Prince's tour manager and a vice-president at Paisley Park until 1992, the three sang all of the lines in harmony at the same time. Later, Prince decided to mix out two voices on each line, leaving one voice to carry the line. It gives the verses a totally different feel, the effect being of a band with strong frontline rather than a well-schooled harmony

team. Jill Jones, a singer who would become increasingly important to Prince's scheme of things in the next few years, also adds her voice.

What they're singing about is music and dance as the route to salvation. On the eve of the year 2000 at the threshold of Armageddon, let's partee! Of course, in 1982 there was still a Cold War, a mind-boggling arsenal of nuclear weapons was still commissioned and targeted ('Mommy, why does everybody have a bomb,' they sing), there was growing fundamentalism in various parts of the world, particularly the Middle East, and the sort of fatalism caused by prolonged meditation on these facts – we'll all die anyway – is transposed to the single-minded desire to dance like it's the last night of the world. It is gallows funk.

'1999' is also the first Prince track which has an epic quality to it. The opening chords are like the accompaniment to a curtain rising, preparing the listener for something special. There's a supreme, bouncy confidence in the funk'n'dance playing which permeates the whole album.

The title track was released as a single in September, 1982, a month before the album. It reached No 44 in the US and in Britain, where it was released in January, 1983, it reached No 25, his first chart placing of any significance outside his homeland.

Little Red Corvette

The second single off the album. It was released in the USA in February, 1983, in the wake of the success of both the album and the increasingly polished live performances, peaking at No 6 in the pop charts. After that date, the racial mix of the audiences at Prince's American shows changed fundamentally from 90 per cent black at the start of the tour, when he was playing smaller theatres, to a split which showed white rock fans in the majority by the end of the tour when he was playing the larger indoor arenas. The promotion videos for the singles off '1999' also forced their way on to MTV, which until Michael Jackson's 'Billie Jean' had an unwritten 'no black music' policy. In the UK, the single was released twice in 1983 but made no chart impact on either occasion. Perhaps the disappointment going

on cynicism sparked by the cancellation of live dates in January and April went some way to explaining the failure.

Prince wrote 'Little Red Corvette' in the back of an Edsel. It has become a part of the canon of car songs which have a long-established place in American rock'n'roll stretching back to early Chuck Berry songs such as 'The Jaguar & The Thunderbird' and 'No Particular Place To Go'. 'Corvette' takes the familiar car-sex metaphor, which typically equates the male sexual drive to the throb of an engine. Equally typically, Prince turns the metaphor on its head. The sporty vehicle belongs to a girl. She's the one with the overdrive, he's on the defensive, most particularly when she drives him to her room decorated with snaps of past conquests. Has you 'got enough gas' to last, she asks him. In fact, this is little more than a classic role reversal done with humour and panache. What sold it was the joyous pop chorus.

Delirious

On the original vinyl album, this track completed the uniformly excellent first side. It's a whizz-bang three-chord rock song taken at a pace somewhere between the jaunty and the demented. But despite a wacky organ sound, it's played crisp and clean. The lyric continues the use of car imagery – wheels, brakes, race, steer and ride all figure – and the situation of the woman in control. Her close proximity induces delirium, he's the helpless victim in thrall of his condition. It struck a chord with a lot of people, though. Released as the third single almost a year after the album's release, 'Delirious' was Prince's second American Top 10 pop hit, reaching No 8. Its B-side, 'Horny Toad', was the first specially recorded as such (previously they'd been other album tracks) and from henceforward he would put new songs on the flips of most of his singles. (See chapter The Hits/The B Sides.)

Let's Pretend We're Married

Delirium has set in for good. 'Let's Pretend' maintains both the pace of 'Delirious' and the picture of the male of the species in love trouble. Ditched by his girlfriend, Prince's only cure is to meet and marry another one in a hurry, preferably by the end of the track although scatological chat such as 'I sincerely want to fuck the taste out of your mouth' may not be the way to a girl's heart. Certainly the vocal is full of throwaway lines – 'all the hippies sing together' and there are doo-wop harmonies and soul screams taken to extremes. Finally exhausted by his delirium, Prince announces that he's off to another life, how about you?

DMSR

That's 'DMSR' as in 'Dance, Music, Sex, Romance', which leaves little in the lyric to explain. These are the things he believes in; 'DMSR' is his credo. Musically, it's good funk. Compared to, say, the heavy funk of George Clinton's Parliafunkadelicment stable, Prince's funk cuts did not bear down quite so heavily but here, though, he begins to get the music funky-dirty – there'd never been any question about the lyrics not being that way inclined. The mesh of keyboards and guitar, mimicked at one point by a drum pattern pattered around tom-toms, help set an insistent tempo behind a funk chant listing the four items on Prince's agenda.

Automatic

Another submissive love song. Utterly besotted, Prince is mesmerised under his lover's command. He'll do anything, everything. He begs for mercy. Recurring keyboards and synthesiser phrases appear in the mid-tempo track and amplify the general state of dependency. This man is in a love-struck trance. What he does, he does robotically. The long instrumental outro, like the wailing of souls in torment, suggests there is no release from his torture.

Something In The Water (Does Not Compute)

A good idea gone bad for reason of deliberate obfuscation. Here, Prince blames the loss of his girlfriend on the water supply. This is the man from 'Delirium' getting really, *really* desperate. When things go wrong in love it is part of human nature to look for external excuses when in fact the answers are often inside us. 'Water' continues the rather Spartan musical arrangement and sound of 'Automatic', where things are also out of Prince's control.

Free

An authentic stadium rock ballad which Prince would later raise to apotheosis with 'Purple Rain', 'Free', sung in falsetto, is a straightforward message to the inhabitants of the land of the free that they should learn to cherish that freedom. The crunch of jackboots marching through city streets and the use of martial snare drumming is an unequivocal warning. This is the sound of life under totalitarian regimes. This is the sound of invasion. Be glad that you are free, he sang.

Lady Cab Driver

The other big car track on '1999' started the fourth and final side of the vinyl release and, despite the title, finds the male back in the metaphorical driving seat. A perky funk rhythm track carries a catchy little melody. So far so dinky. The storyline is a whole other fare. Woman cabbie picks up Prince whose emotions and very soul are in turmoil. Inverting the earlier scenarios in which he's the submissive one, he seduces the driver, played by Jill Jones, to comfort him in the back seat of her cab. They couple noisily, squealingly. As the lovemaking intensifies he dedicates each thrust, at first to objects of his anger, hate or jealousy, later to those he loves (notably God and women). It was, in 1982, a risky and audacious track by any stretch of the imagination. The fairly wild guitar solo was the only way to climax the track; Chic-like chicken scratch chords ease the track down.

All The Critics Love U In New York

You can dance if you want to, Prince suggests, probably tongue in cheek because this track rattles along like an express train. It certainly conveys some sense of the pace of New York, where everything can be there for the asking if the crits are good. Although Prince was getting many more good reviews than bad he's not about to give *them* a good Press. Moreover, everyone in the Big Apple's a critic, right? Prince cranks up into a heavy metal guitar solo, warns off punks and hippies alike and generally lays about him in a fit of pique.

International Lover

Sex and travel. This most potent combination has fuelled a good proportion of '1999' and gives the album its rousing finale. A slow song. The all-seeing, all-knowing, all-satisfying narrator/lover boards his seduction 747 'fully equipped with everything your body desires'. Among the many plays with words and situations associated with air travel he appears to have missed the phrase Intercoital Airlines. As he hands out membership of the mile high club there is a lot more panting, gasping and screaming. As with the final track on 'Controversy' ('Jack U Off'), he used this final cut as the framework for the most lascivious moments of the '1999' stage show, stripping down and mounting a brass bed, though he is in no mood for sleep.

PURPLE RAIN

(FIRST RELEASE JUNE, 1984 US VINYL WARNER BROS 25110-1, CD 25110-2.
UK WEA 925110-1, CD 925110-2.)

While he was on the 1999 tour, Prince spent many spare moments jotting ideas into a purple notebook. Mainstream was on his mind. Some ideas would turn into an album that presented a broader range of rock styles – it was not a very funky record – and dealt predominantly with much less controversial subjects than on any of the preceding albums. Some of the notes he made were for songs for other acts. And some were for another project which had been germinating in his mind – a full length feature film. He made it a condition for signing a new management contract with Cavallo, Ruffalo & Fargnoli – the deal was due for renegotiation – that they'd fix him up with a movie deal.

Rock musicians have rarely made incandescent movie stars. Elvis Presley made a lot of films but, no matter how often they are 'reassessed' by film buffs, they were mostly dire. The films of the Fifties, which tried to explain and exploit the rock 'n' roll boom, featured either uncomfortable singers in cameo roles plugging their latest hit or mediocre actors becoming mediocre pop singers, all very kitsch. The Beatles films in the Sixties had, through the zany direction of Richard Lester, captured something of the spirit of the times. In the Seventies one saw the occasional concert or festival movie, the film of The Who's 'Tommy' and 'Saturday Night Fever',

spawned by the disco-boom but inadequate to it, existing merely as a vehicle for John Travolta and for The Bee Gees' music. Few rock stars acquitted themselves well on-screen. And, bottom line, Diana Ross's portrayal of Billie Holiday aside, African-American singers were invisible as potential bankable Hollywood stars. And who, in Hollywood terms, was Prince? He'd only just broken through to the mass rock audience at the fifth attempt. His only celluloid credentials were a few videos and the fact that he was as small as Alan Ladd.

His managers had little encouragement when they approached the film studios for

fired me' – and was replaced by Wendy Melvoin, a friend of Lisa Coleman. She'd travelled with the band for part of the 1999 tour. Jimmy 'Jam' Harris and Terry Lewis had their first hit as producers ('Just Be Good To Me' by the SOS Band) and quit The Time to concentrate on their Flyte Tyme production company. Jam & Lewis became an important chapter in the story of the Minneapolis sound, refining it further through their work with Alexander O'Neal and Janet Jackson, among many others. Finally, just a matter of weeks before filming was due to start, Vanity quit her group and the film. Patricia Kotero, renamed Apollonia, replaced her in the film and, as the nipple-count in the trio remained the same, the group became Apollonia 6.

financing. Even Warner Bros, the record company's much larger film production corporation, were dubious. So the managers put in some of their own money, got a loan from Warner Bros and independent finance from elsewhere and as soon as the 1999 tour ended, Prince and selected members of the entourage, including The Time and Vanity 6, went into six months of concentrated lessons in acting and dancing.

Dez Dickerson had left the band at the end of the tour – 'if I'd have been [Prince] I'd have

Back in pre-production, screenwriter William Blinn, working with Prince, wrote a screenplay based on Prince's life as he knew it. He saw the singer's relationship with his father as the motor that drove him. The emphasis on sex was somewhat heavier than in the version which became the shooting script. While working on the script, Prince continued to write new music at a phenomenal rate. Some songs made the soundtrack, some were reworked for other artists – Jill Jones, Apollonia 6 – and some never surfaced officially.

The penurious company providing Prince and entourage with dance classes, the Minnesota Dance Theatre, persuaded the leader to do a benefit concert in the Twin Cities which raised $23,000. The show, recorded live, featured the début by Wendy Melvoin in several new songs, three of which, 'Purple Rain', 'I Would Die 4 U' and 'Baby, I'm A Star', went straight into the film as basic tracks. When Blinn finished his second draft of the script he went back to his 'day' job, executive producer of the TV series based on *Fame*, and Prince's management signed Albert Magnoli to direct the film. He set about rewriting the script. Although it is not an accurate film biography, there is no doubt that the film is based on relationships in Minneapolis. Morris Day, the extrovert lead singer of The Time, is quite obviously playing himself.

Costing $7m, the movie was shot in 10-weeks on location in Minneapolis starting in November, 1983. Because of the cold, several scenes had to be shot in the first couple of months of 1984. Prince, naturally, was between times still recording – The Time's third album, 'Ice Cream Castles', was to be their last for over half a decade and there were débuts for Apollonia 6 and Sheila E (Escovedo).

The release of the 'Purple Rain' album in June, 1984, a month before the film, was the best publicity the movie could have. Prince knew he had recorded the big cross-over album according to recording engineer Susan Rogers. 'He was ecstatic,' when the album was completed. 'Purple Rain' sold a million within days and was the No 1 album in the USA for over six months. It sold 10 million copies in America, half that number around the rest of the world. The film did just as well – rave reviews, followed by a $70m gross, 10 times the initial investment.

In line with the movie, in which Prince played The Kid, leader of The Revolution, the best band in town locked in rivalry until the final encore with Morris Day's band, the album was credited as produced, arranged, composed and performed by Prince & The Revolution.

Although he was still the main contributor, this was a first acknowledgement of the effort of the band as a unit. Previously he had appeared to be the sole creator and sparingly credited individual musicians on a track by track basis. This departure was sensible as publicity for the movie, but also a sensitive move in recognition of the development of the band under his direction throughout the 1999 tour.

The album sleeve is a return to portrait – Prince perched on the motorcycle, eyeing the camera with a mixture of mischief and challenge, a woman in the doorway behind him. Adorning the bike is the blended male/female symbols just a refinement away from becoming his first sign of the times. On the back sleeve is scrawled a piece of purple prose drawing on scenes in the film. It's the moony sort of seduction chit-chat indulged in by teenage lovers before real life impinges. Or by profoundly incurable romantics. The text is set against a carpet of blooms. On the inner sleeve, the lyrics and credits, all scripted in purple and printed atop a dark photograph of evening sunlight on water, are a great trial to read.

Let's Go Crazy

Musical, drama and dance rehearsals for the film were held in the Warehouse, in Eden Prairie, 15 miles outside Minneapolis. Super-confident in the band, Prince had his recording equipment ripped out of his studio and installed at the Warehouse to record the rehearsals. Instruments leaked from one track to the next, there was interference from other apparatus but ultimately, the tracks were good enough, and had the electric presence of 'live' performance, to be used on the 'Purple Rain' album. 'Crazy' was one of them. A rock romp, it opens with 'churchy' organ chords and a sermon, which accurately monitors the cadences of a Baptist preacher – 'Dearly beloved, we are gathered here today to get through this thing called life,' he intones, adding the promise of a better after-life. But in the meantime, to get through this world of toil and strife without recourse to Dr. Everythingllbealright, the Beverly Hills shrink, let's 'party'! 'He's comin',' Prince whispers, 'He's comin',' and for once does not mean ejaculation. It's not too far from the apocalyptic content of '1999' but that track's funk is replaced by a hard, effervescent pop-rock, heavy on guitars. (Interestingly, on 'The Hits Collection' '1999' is sequenced to follow 'Crazy'.) The second single off the album, it was released at the same time as the film and shot to No 1 in the USA.

Take Me With U

A mid-tempo pop love song shaped by acoustic guitar, the 'straightest' arrangement on the album and, probably as a result, the least interesting track. It was recorded in the Sunset Sound studio in Los Angeles. Apollonia shares the vocal on a lyric describing a yearning for a love of complete selflessness. It works better in the movie as accompaniment to their bike ride through the countryside.

The Beautiful Ones

A ballad, sung falsetto, it's one of only three tracks on 'Purple Rain' which feature Prince as Mr. DIY. It was also recorded at Sunset Sound in Los Angeles. The lyric is again driven by a craving for companionship and love and a maudlin fatalism about the beautiful ones (in

terms of personality as well as looks) who always seem to lose in love. He attacks the song *hard* at the end, like a berserk soul singer, though his screams of pain and desire actually begin to sound rather petulant by the end.

Computer Blue

Co-written with Lisa Coleman, Wendy Melvoin, Matt Fink and his father, John L Nelson, 'Computer Blue' was also record at the Warehouse in the summer of 1983. Opening with a conversation between 'wendynlisa', who by now had become a virtually inseparable, somewhat mysterious and enigmatic female pairing in the band, the song develops on a squarely driven 4/4 rhythmic platform with the computer/Prince wondering what's happened to a love life. After a pop guitar solo, the track slows to a lope and segues into...

Darling Nikki

The one track on 'Purple Rain' which might raise eyebrows and hackles among the moral majority but produces a warm glow of recognition among those who could plot his recording career as a series of brief dalliances with insatiable women in well-equipped apartments. The second all-Prince track, it somewhat leeringly tells the tale of a girl he first met in a hotel lobby 'masturbating with a magazine', as one does, of course. It was recorded, the sleeve credits cryptically note, 'at a place close to where u live'. The taped voice played backward towards the end of the track repeats the uplifting message from 'Let's Go Crazy': 'He is coming, He is coming'.

When Doves Cry

The first single off the album, released in May, 1984, it quickly became his first US No 1 and at two million copies was the biggest selling single of the year. Recorded at Sunset Sound, 'Doves' was the final cut on the album for which Prince took all credits. Like a piece of Jimi Hendrix grandstanding, the tracks starts with a guitar solo and is set against a loud, sol-

id and punchy 4/4 drum pattern and no bass. The drums and drum machines carry the instrumental burden entirely, with a few percussive keyboard phrases and interjections. The multi-track vocals cut to the essence of his personality. He's in love but he fusses and fights, despairs of those parts of his personality which seem like his mother's and father's. Equating the noise of birds of peace fighting to the sound of a lovers' spat is a particularly effective image.

I Would Die 4 U

The basic tracks for the final three songs on the album were taped on the hoof when Prince unexpectedly decided to record the benefit show in aid of the Minnesota Dance Theatre at the First Avenue. In terms of pure purple pop, it's a simple melody in 4/4 time but the snare picks up only alternate on-beats, leaving the fourth beat in every bar free or filled by a synthesised handclap. This gives the snappy pop-rock pace a frisson of funk. The lyric is a metaphysical expression of utter devotion. He starts by offering to be her lover and friend, but he has the potential to become much more – her messiah.

Baby, I'm A Star

A fast, raving rocker, 'Star' is the climax of the film's last concert with Prince locked tight in the spotlight. A terrific stage number, it is a profoundly, flamboyantly, confident adrenalin rush, the pure sound of star material, which can be found in the drawer marked 'Narcissism'. It also sounds like something crafted for The Time's Morris Day in his most preening mood.

Purple Rain

Chiming guitars and steady drumming introduce a great – as in epic – rock anthem. The thick, textured guitar-based chords wash across the track like a misty rain against an ever expanding soundscape. And, what do we know, Prince had never wanted to be the girl's lover, he only wanted to be a friend. We all change, life goes on, as individuals we develop at different speeds and move in different directions. But some of us stay friends for life. Prince has become *very* philosophical in a way that his earlier persona would not recognise.

Like most rock songs of the genus Stadia Rockitis Anthemata, the arrangement of the long fade is intrinsically and powerfully manipulative in the way it pulls responses from listeners. One has heard this type of repetitive singalong – rhythmically slow and swaying, melodically simple – many times before and, like Pavlov's dog, knows what is expected. As stadium anthems go, 'Purple Rain' is one of the most affecting and effective. Cue swaying hordes, cue lighted candles, roll credits. The purple reigned.

AROUND THE WORLD IN A DAY

(FIRST RELEASE APRIL, 1985. US VINYL PAISLEY PARK/WARNERS BROS 25286-1, CD 25286-2; UK WEA 925286-1, CD 925286-2.)

The first release on Paisley Park, Prince's own label. Prince once told *Rolling Stone* that he did outrageous things not to shock but because no-one else would dare to do them. Although not shocking in the sexual sense, as had usually been the case, 'Around The World' was certainly not the expected follow-up. This was not 'Purple Rain: The Sequel'. In the seven years since 'For You', there had been very clear and identifiable organic growth in Prince's music. It trod a path through black pop, funk and finally into the mainstream rock terrain of 'Rain'. His lyrics had by turns intrigued, outraged, puzzled and amused. He'd developed an extremely tight live show full of visual impact and musical flash, and play-acting and posturing. And he had made a smash movie.

In April, 1985 the 'Purple Rain' album was still in the Top 20, Prince & The Revolution were still on tour supporting the album and film, and the video of the movie was on *that* chart when *Billboard* announced that Warner Bros were preparing to ship the next Prince studio album. At the time (March, 1985), the magazine said that no single was planned. In fact, 'Paisley Park' had been scheduled for release on February 27 but was withdrawn, possibly to avoid a clash with the multi-artist 'We Are The World', released in aid of the USA for Africa charity, in which Prince had declined to take part. (He contributed a track, '4 The Tears In Your Eyes', to the album.) Although rock bands, like Led Zeppelin in the UK, had long eschewed singles, it was unusual for acts with proven pop appeal to do this. The Beatles' release of 'Sgt Pepper's Lonely Hearts Club Band' was the obvious precedent. This was to be significant.

Most of 'Around The World' had, in fact, been recorded in the time between the 'Purple Rain' album and tour. At the same time he was also putting together songs for an album by The Family (the remnants of The Time after Messers Day, Jam, Lewis and Monte Moir had quit), which he would record virtually as a solo album but under the group's banner, in April, 1985 just as 'Around The World' was being released. He would have been best advised, if he was taking advice at all at this time, which seems improbable, to have edited the material more rigorously and combined the best songs into one album. 'Around The World' sounded insubstantial at the time of its release and the passing of the years has leant no great charm to songs which at the time sounded deeply dippy, though a few tracks remain likeable enough in the album's context.

The warning bells began ringing loud and clear when Prince announced that the new album was 'a personal statement'. Who needs telling? The best music is almost always the result of the utterance of 'a personal statement' of the objective observations or subjective feelings by an artist on a given topic or incident.

As an effort to elucidate a personal philosophy, 'Around The World' is a failure. It has all the clarity, logic and perspicacity of a religious cult's credo. Its visionary brew is a mixture of post-hippy, fuzzy-brained rambling and Prince's continuing attempt to reconcile his life as it was and is with a deeper yearning for spiritual fulfilment, which he hopes to find in an ongoing conversation with God. All well and Christian, of course, but at this precise point it is unlikely that God knows what his supplicant is on about.

Musically, the album is almost entirely shorn of African-American style. Bye-bye black market. The mainstream rock audience, so totally won over by 'Purple Rain', will also have been perplexed by the experimentations here. Although the use of exotic instrumentation was scarcely novel in rock, Prince was probably inducting a new audience in the sounds of the oud, finger cymbal and darbuka

After its release, Prince told *Rolling Stone* that he had not wanted to make 'an album like the earlier ones'. In this respect, he was entirely successful. The album reached No 1 in the USA, selling three million; around the world, sales reached 1.2 million In the UK, the album reached No 5.

Around The World In A Day

What promises to be a magic carpet ride quickly becomes lost in the narrow streets of the bazaar. Written by Prince with his father and David Coleman, the track starts instrumentally in the Middle East amid whistles, bells, pipes, thuds (the darbuka), flutes and creates the atmosphere of a chaotic procession – through the crowded soul of Prince's mind, one is tempted to add. Open your hearts and minds, Prince advises us. Thereafter, the magical mystery tour – where has one heard that before? – takes a wrong turning. The title-line provides a catchy refrain but the rest of the lyric, with its transcendental vision of, among other things, children gambolling in Elysian fields, might have been written in 1969. The brief, belated switch into a dance groove is effective.

Paisley Park

Paisley Park is not in Minneapolis. It is the state of knowledge and harmony that resides within all of us. *He* does not have the answer, Prince has said, he is not 'a visionary'. So, without using the word karma, we are encour-aged to seek our Paisley Parks within us to the accompaniment of a very merry little song. The melody, vocal and rhythm arrangements and production values resonate to the sound of The Beatles as do portions of the lyrics, particularly images like 'a girl on a see-saw' and lonely wives. Paisley Park, a place where there are no rules, could as well be San Francisco, 1969 as in the mind of Minneapolis's best-known son, 1985 – except for Prince's well-known stance against drugs and drink, of course. In late May the track was released as the first UK single off the album and reached No 17.

Condition Of The Heart

There is a potentially lovely ballad here lost somewhere in the baroque ornamentation that passes for an arrangement. Occasionally it escapes for a breath of fresh air but too often it is buried in ambitious orchestration, which only blurs the song's focus. The piece is indicative of the lack of editing on the album. Like the entire album, the track could be a wee joke, lampooning the over-wrought ballads with which rock singers intersperse their shows to show versatility and sensitivity. If so, bullseye.

Raspberry Beret

One of the two obvious pop hits on the album and a return to the straighter narrative of his earlier writing, it jumps off the record as if to say 'Hi! Remember me! It's Prince! Had y'all fooled?' He's working in a store, girl walks in, instant love, on to the motorcycle and off to the countryside again, for anyone who had forgotten his rides in the 'Purple Rain' movie. He quite often uses a string section on 'Around The World' and 'Beret' features one of the simplest and most effective arrangements. Released as a single in the USA in May, 1985, it reached No 2, his seventh pop Top 10 hit. In the UK it went to No 25 in July.

Tamborine

A very slight piece structurally (on the one funk which, after the first few bars, never gives the rhythm its due prominence), melodically and lyrically as it descends into a rather silly, sniggering song about seeing a girl's face in a magazine, falling in love and staying at home all day to play with his tamborine. Yuk, yuk.

America

On vinyl and cassette, this track opened the second side and promised better things to come. As it cranks up, a rock guitar takes on 'America The Beautiful' in the manner of Jimi Hendrix's 'Star Spangled Banner' leading into the full, blasting 4/4 uptempo charge with a funky-butt bass-line. The message here is that kids are the future of all nations, and that the country had better look out for theirs a lot better than they were doing at present. But it's still the best country in the world, look at the alternatives. It's a song one would have liked to hear his well-drilled band vamp on for a while longer and, because they don't, is illustrative of the hurried and unfinished feeling given off by much of the album. Released in October, 1985 as the third American single off the album, it reached No 46.

Pop Life

By far the most accessible track on the album, 'Pop Life' moves at a good, steady walkin' pace set up by Sheila E's drumming. Read

superficially, the lyric urges everyone to be
happier with their lot, to take a more positive
pleasure in the person they are and the things
that they have rather than coveting their neighbour's possessions or position. It's shot
through with positive one liners – about staying in school, not wasting money on drugs,
being satisfied with one's appearance – but
whether these add up to a cohesive game plan
for life in the late 20th century is debatable.
The sentiments are arguably very unAmerican,
which is ironic coming after the patriotic fer-
vour of the previous track. It went to No 7 in
the US and as the third UK single, No 60.

The Ladder

It apparently came as much of a shock to his
management as to the audience when he
announced after the final encore of the final
Purple Rain tour date (Orange Bowl, Miami,
April 7, 1985) that he was retiring from live
performance for a while. He was, he later
explained, going to look for the ladder. Little
did we know that it was here for all to hear
Co-written with his father, 'The Ladder' starts
as a parable of a mythical king seeking spiritual

enlightenment. As the choir of Wendy, Lisa, Susannah Melvoin and Taja Sevelle steadily build a gospel feel with Eddie M's exultant sax weaving and wailing throughout, Prince sings that this is the process we all go through when confronting The Meaning of Life. How did it begin? How will it end? The slow, heavy plod of the track's rhythm, like a man labouring up steep steps, and the way the track fades wailing on suggests that he at least is still searching.

Temptation

'Sex... Temptation... Lust' Prince interjects through a wall of metal guitar before this rocker settles into a mid-tempo groove. No sooner has the spiritual Prince started climbing the ladder than his earthly body plunges back into the hot, fetid swamp of base human passions. Here is a track made for him to roll around to on stage with Eddie M's squealing sax for company. This is the nitty gritty sex of early albums. But there is penance in the final moments when, after what sounds like a Hieronymous Bosch painting set to music, God appears and threatens to provide swift proof of the singer's mortality. He apologises in the manner of a naughty child caught stealing apples from an orchard rather than a true repentant. 'Love is more important than sex, now I understand. I have to go now. I don't know when I'll return'. Even though irony does not seem to feature over much in the Prince songbook, it is hard to believe that he is not being so here.

PRINCE AND THE

PARADE

(FIRST RELEASE MARCH, 1986. US VINYL PAISLEY PARK/WARNER BROS 25395-1, CD 25395-2. UK WEA 925395-1, CD 925395-2.)

With 'Around The World', Prince had utterly confounded the critics and marketing department of his record company who so like to categorise acts. How do you compartmentalise this writer, singer, musician, arranger, producer who can do funk, pop and rock so well, who steadfastly refuses to stay in one bag and, moreover, who variously infuses tracks with shadings of gospel, psychedelia, jazz and other forms?

Of course, categorisation has its uses, not least, it must be said, for those artists who enrich themselves by milking a particular sector dry while bemoaning the fact that they are restricted by the demands of that sector. Although at first Prince was marketed as a black pop act, his risque lyrics spoke to the rock magazines, who helped to broaden his appeal quickly and to gain a foothold in the rock market. But it had to be there in the grooves first. Then, in terms of exposure and raising awareness, the 'Purple Rain' movie did in a year what might normally take an African-American artist 10 years to achieve. It is typical of Prince that he chose not to consolidate this in the accepted way – by creating an accessible follow-up. Instead, he gave a personal statement. (What were the six albums before it?)

There are some critics who rate Prince's eighth album among his finest works. Given the cluttered experimentation which drove him into the *cul de sac* of 'Around The World', it is certainly a significant improvement. He's back on the straight and narrow of developing his music in a more linear fashion, though some essence of 'Around The World' remains. Just as that album confounded the industry and critics with its music, 'Parade' was a shock simply because it was there – his third album in less than two years. (Three albums would last most established acts for at least five years.)

There was 'no concern from me about burn out', Warner Bros' then vice president of sales Lou Dennis told *Billboard*. 'Following up a big, big record is always a problem. Who knows how long the proper amount of time to wait between superstar releases is? In some cases, I think these artists take too long.' (His company was tapping its toes on an overdue Madonna album.)

Word from Prince's organisation was the same. 'You can't make blanket rules,' Alan Leeds said to the same trade magazine. 'You have to approach an artist as an artist, examining their way of operating, audience demographic, music and goals. What works for Michael Jackson doesn't work for Prince and *vice versa*. Prince isn't the kind of artist who looks at the calendar and says 'It's time to write'. He's a free-form artist and a free-form business man. He makes music first, then considers how to market it. He has never done anything by the rules in any area of the business.

Until 'Purple Rain', the longest gap between any album had been a year. Between '1999' and 'Rain' there were 20 months but in that time he made a film, recorded many other artists, toured and still wrote. Hence the backlog of material.

'Parade' featured music from his second movie *Under The Cherry Moon*, over which it is perhaps best to draw a discreet veil. In decades to come, the film, directed by its star, may become a collectable piece of kitsch, cherished for its awfulness. Shot between September-November, 1985 in the south of France, which one hopes gave the cast a pleasant if not inexpensive few weeks on the Mediterranean, the story follows the exploits of philanderers Prince and Jerome Benton (one time Morris Day 'valet' and later a Prince singer-dancer) chasing moneyed women on the Riviera until True Love cuts the diminutive gigolo down to size. Rare episodes of backchat between Prince and Benton aside, the movie, shot in black-and-white to make the least of the locations, is a forgettable and ineffectual piece of tosh. The music is better.

Recorded, again, at the favoured locations of Paisley Park and Sunset Sound, 'Parade' had 12 songs, seven on the first side, titled 'Intro', of the vinyl release and five on the second, 'End'. During the filming of *Cherry Moon*, The Revolution had acquired several permanent members. Guitarist Miko Weaver, a for-

Coleman, Wendy Melvoin and Brown Mark, The Revolution was now an 11-piece. The horns, particularly, were a blast. New versions of old songs replaced synthesiser lines with 'real' horns and the with the advantage of brevity, the arrangements and juiced-up pace gave the music a fresh integral drive. On record, he also started to use a full string section to increase the colours available. Clare Fischer wrote and arranged the orchestra's parts.

The shows swerved away from the rock of 'Rain' to a harder, funkier sound with Prince, freed from playing guitar by the addition of Weaver, taking a more mobile, physical role. This was a genuine rock 'n' soul revue which no longer had a standard set but plucked songs to fit the mood from a formidable songbook.

'Parade' was a No 3 hit album in the USA and sold 1.8m, possibly a consequence of disappointment with 'Around The World'. It sold almost as many outside the States – 1.4m – and got to No 4 in the UK. And, although the album was an immediate and firm favourite with many critics, only one track turns up on

mer Sheila E band man, and saxophonist Eric Leeds, the younger brother of Prince's 'Purple Rain' tour manager Alan, had played on those shows. He suggested his friend, trumpeter friend Matt Blistan, later known as Atlanta Bliss, when Prince decided to further expand his brass section. This added a kaleidoscope of new musical colours to his soundscape and would affirm his reputation as an excellent band organiser. For the 'show' part of the business, he added Benton, Greg Brooks and Wally Safford as singers-dancers. With the existing five-piece of Bobby Z, Matt Fink, Lisa

'The Hits'. Prince shared credits with his father on two songs; full string, brass and woodwind sections are credited.

Christopher Tracy's Parade

The name of his character in *Cherry Moon*, CT's 'Parade' was co-written by John L Nelson. Every conceivable instrument and sound, plus the kitchen sink, *with* echo seems to be used. Effectively a link back to 'Around The World' because it has the sound, feel and ambition of the Beatles *circa* 1967, the track spreads out to become a 'big' sound, like the march of a circus band parading through town announcing the arrival of the big top. The lyrics, sung in a tone that would not be out of place reciting a nursery-rhyme, are equally wide-eyed. It segues in to...

New Position

An up-front and in yo' face drum sound is at the core of this industrial clatter of a funk 'n' dance groove. The arrangement is a stripped down lean machine, totally without upholstery and precision-tuned for the pelvis and feet. Its

efficiency is almost Germanic. The lyric's most appealing phrase? 'Let's go fishing in the sea of life.' And why should he want to do that? Because his sex life's at a low ebb and needs new input. The pulse of the track slows and segues via laughter, presumably he found the new position, into...

I Wonder U

Steel pans, a booming bass drum and the suggestion of horns, leads into a short piece of under two minutes which hyphenates 'Christopher Tracy's Parade' and the next song. Despite the rich tone and full sound from the varied instrumentation there is a messy, unfinished quality to the track. It segues into...

Under The Cherry Moon

The second song on the album to be co-written by Prince *et* Pere, it does homage to his father's calling with a prominent jazz piano part. It is a fairly melancholic piece, again more impressive for the broad sweep of the sound it creates than the actual effect of the finished product. In common with other film scores, it needs the accompaniment of the images for which it was written. Divorced from them, it seems incomplete.

Girls & Boys

Fun time in La Belle France. A throw back to his earlier style which mixed light funk and catchy pop, this is a breezy, capricious work-out with a repetitive, whimsical little five-note keyboard phrase later picked up by Leeds's sax which takes the feel back to sixties soul. Les girls– Lisa and Wendy, Sheila E and Susannah Melvoin – track his lead vocal. Later on his clothes designer, Marie France, has a talk-on role as a French seductress. It was released as a single in the UK in August, 1986 and reached No 11. In the USA it appeared only as a B-side.

Life Can Be So Nice

Loud, thwacking drums preface a booming funk track. The on-the-one funk device of let-ting the first downbeat of the 4\4 bar reverber-ate to the last upbeat is much in evidence as Prince spins and whirls through his paces. But interlaced with the African-American influence

is, again, a pop-rock sensibility. Intriguing though the stew of textures is, the ultimate feeling is one of a slightly messy and confused track. It is strange that one so adept at rehearsing, organising and confidently leading a band on stage, on a couple of occasions in 'Parade' fails to get to grips with the recording. Perhaps the pressure of work on the film – its failure at the box office he would put down to directing something he had not written – was proving more stressful than he'd realised. 'Life Can Be So Nice' is cut-off in full flow with the severity of a guillotine.

Venus de Milo

After the rattle and hum of the previous track, this is a peaceful instrumental, quite cinematic, performed on acoustic piano with a string section.

Mountains

Opening the second side of the vinyl release, 'Mountains' was the second American single from the album and reached No 23. ('Alexa de Paris', its B-side, appeared in the film but not on 'Parade' or on the 'B-sides' portions of

'The Hits/B-Sides' triple CD collection.) Played over the closing titles to the film, 'Mountains' is a loud and confident mid-tempo meshing of funk and rock in strict and solid 4/4 time. Eric Leeds's horn is again prominent in the mix as Prince equates his powerful love to Mother Nature as defined by the mountains and the sea. In a *Rolling Stone* piece, it was alleged that Wendy & Lisa were co-writers of 'Mountains' with Prince. They are not credited as such.

Do U Lie?

An adventurous cut which again takes on board some musical baggage from the continent on which he was filming *Cherry Moon*. Prince, back in distrusting mood and falsetto pitch, starts 'Do U Lie?' in the mood of a chanson, accordion and all, and later slips into something more comfortable, namely swing-time, sliding in on bass guitar. Sandra Francisco takes the role of gypsy waif.

Kiss

Although the album credits David Z merely as arranger, the drummer and Revolution's bassist Brown Mark had the germ of the track as a demo for the Paisley Park band Mazarati. They couldn't do anything with it so Prince got hold of it, gave it a groove and finished it. Even then, it was added to 'Parade' as a second thought and, according to Alan Leeds, Prince was never fully convinced that it belonged on the record.

Nonetheless, commercially it was the album's most successful track. Released as a single a month-and-a-half before the album, it was his third No 1 US single and reached No

6 in the UK. The cut opens with a brief chicken-scratch guitar chording, signature of James Brown's funk. It reappears at the end of every verse, like the hook in 'Papa's Got A Brand New Bag', a grace note of acknowledgement that this is where funk came in.

Singing in falsetto against a simple drums-and-keyboard background, Prince is in the mood for monogamy and devotion. The track moves into solid funk overdrive when the guitar chords and solos ('little girl Wendy's gonna play' he sings) in a sparse, under-stated dance-funk twirl. The guitar actually seems to *dance* . After the ambition and adventure of most of the rest of 'Parade', the simplicity and drive and good feeling of 'Kiss' shines like a beacon.

Anotherloverholenyohead

As in 'you need another lover like you need a hole in your head', this was the third single off the album in the USA, reaching No 63 on the Hot 100. In the UK, it reached No 36. The rhythm track puts greater weight on the snare drum up-beats; the rock guitars crank up in the background suggesting a rock song trying to get out of what might almost pass for a Stevie Wonder early-to-mid-seventies pop-R&B track. But I doubt whether Wonder would have used piano to keep dislocating the flow of the rhythm or the logic of the melody and arrangement. As such, the disjointed flow catches Prince's state of desperation.

Sometimes It Snows In April

The second track on the album alleged, in *Rolling Stone*, to have been co-written by Wendy and Lisa. Piano, guitar and vocals create a picture of, well, a hushed snowfall. The gentle atmosphere thus cleverly and carefully constructed becomes a requiem for Christopher Tracy, Prince's character in the film, who after a fairly amoral existence finds love and pays for it with his life. The ending of the film left one with little sympathy for any of the characters dead or alive. But this song, if anything could, might make one reconsider. It's a sad and genuinely touching lament about loss, described by mature, sensitive lyrics interpreted by a believable and 'straight' vocal delivery.

SIGN 'O' THE TIMES

(FIRST RELEASE MARCH, 1987 US VINYL PAISLEY PARK/WARNER BROS 25577-1, CD 25577-2; UK WEA WX 88 925577-1, CD 925577-2.)

The indefatigable energy with which Prince had been pursuing his career wherever it might take him showed no sign of exhaustion. Quite the contrary as he hit yet another new vein of productivity. His next album evolved throughout 1986, involving no less than four changes of heart in little over nine months while he was also recording three other acts, playing live dates and promoting a film.

After the failure of 'Cherry Moon' and the sluggish sales of 'Parade' in the USA, it might have been prudent to step back a while and take a long, cool, clear look at the direction of the music. No chance. In the spring of 1986, while editing *Cherry Moon* for release, he was also working at Sunset Sound with The Revolution on tracks for a projected double album tentatively titled 'Dream Factory'. There were new songs written with the rest of the band, notably Wendy and Lisa, and some reworked older pieces going back three years. The mix was funk and pop, nothing too heavy. Much of the recording was well-advanced when he set the tracks aside until the tour to promote 'Parade' and the release of *Cherry Moon* had been and gone. Incidentally, the enthusiasm of the film company for the latter can be gauged by the fact that they allowed the location for the July 1 world premiere to be decided in an MTV competition. It was won by a young woman in Sheridan, Wyoming, a town of 10,000 souls in the north of the state close to the Montana border. Probably not a hotbed of Princemania.

By the end of July, Prince had decided to abandon 'Dream Factory' indefinitely – tracks would appear on albums by various Paisley Park acts in the course of the next five years – and he started on another album, 'Crystal Ball', at Sunset Sound. It marked a return to the original format of 'written, arranged, performed and produced' by him alone. At the same time he was also either writing, producing and playing on tracks for a new Sheila E album and the débuts of Jill Jones, the singer who'd first appeared on '1999', and Madhouse, a jammin' jazz-funk-rock band led by saxophonist Eric Leeds. This aggregation of Leeds's former Atlanta colleagues was an ill-disguised cover for more Prince music in a less commercial style.

He had a third change of heart about his own music in 1986 when, in October, he started yet another project under an assumed name, Camille. Again this used new material and older works, including a reject from '1999', and was defined by a return to much tougher and more rigorously arranged funk and harder-edged rock tracks. Working with Leeds, Atlanta Bliss and Madhouse also gave Prince a greater confidence in his use of horns. It informs his best music in the late eighties, confirming his stature as the outstanding bandleader of his generation, the James Brown of the eighties and nineties.

Prince's fourth change of heart was to return to the 'Crystal Ball' tracks, add the best of the 'Camille' tracks and record some more in the basement of his new house at Chanhassen, a rural location roughly 20 miles south-west of Minneapolis where the new

Paisley Park studio had been under construction since March, 1986. This putative triple album reached mastering stage before being edited down to a double album, a late addition to the running order becoming its title track. The tracks which had been lost when 'Crystal Ball', the triple, became 'Sign 'O' The Times', the double, were going to be released as 'Camille', a single album, but this plan was shelved. There was already a feast of new music available by Prince and associates (he was also recording with the marvellous soul-gospel singer Mavis Staples and with the wizard of funk, George Clinton) and Warners promotion budget would stretch only so far. By June, 1986, Prince was telling a radio interviewer that he had 320 tracks recorded and ready to roll.

Then he announced that Wendy, Lisa and Bobby Z had left The Revolution. In fact, he sacked them. The two women launched a recording career together; Bobby Z returned to producing. Brown Mark also left, slightly later and under his own steam, to begin recording as a solo act.

It's apparent that whatever the disadvantages or restrictions, a musician's life with Prince was never dull or indolent. On stage, too, he wanted his players to be more alert and able to adapt to the quick instructions he'd give – with a shout, wave of the hand or toss of the head – to change the tempo of a song, to cut to a bridge, to vamp, to segue into another song, to interpolate part of one song into another. One view is, that for Prince's new purposes, The Revolution couldn't cut it as a unit. Whatever, by the end of 1986, only Matt Fink of the original band remained. The horn section of Leeds and Atlanta Bliss, guitarist Miko Weaver and singer/dancers Greg Brooks and Wally Safford stayed on board. Sheila E joined as drummer and the bassist and keyboard players from her band – Levi Seacer Jr and Boni Boyer respectively – were recruited. Cathy Glover, Cat, joined as choreographer/dancer/singer having organised the dancing on several videos by other Paisley Park acts.

Produced, arranged and, predominantly, written and performed by Prince, 'Sign' was, like the previous double album '1999', another high point in his recording career. When he's really burning, feverish with ideas, as he obviously was when laying down the 16 tracks here, the sureness of his touch in every style marks him apart from the dilettante, musical tourist. This is deep-rooted, thoroughly and instinctively understood stuff. 'Purple Rain' might be the biggest seller, but for cohesive artistic vision and achievement, '1999' and 'Sign 'O' The Times' are by some distance his best works.

Of course, both have portions which do not quite work, which fail to hold the attention and pall quickly. But return to them, and they will offer more. And the majority of the music on both albums contains sustained passages of funk and more concise pop songs which have not diminished in attraction over the years. Like all good music, they stand examination in any era, and against any prevailing fashion. '1999' and 'Sign' both draw a line under a particular stage of his development and point the way forward.

The album's sleeve finds Prince, in the bottom right hand corner of the shot, walking off the stage set for the 'Sign' tour. This was a vivid evocation of uptown at night – urgent, bright-flashing neon lights offering food, drink, rooms, girls, games, loans, plus an urban sprawl of wrecked cars and bric-a-brac decorated with gaily strewn wild flowers. It's at least four years since he was last in this territory but he makes it his again. But despite its broad sweep of styles and the solid confidence of his playing, the album sold as relatively poorly in the US – 1.8m – as 'Parade' and reached No 6 on the album chart. He'd failed to carry with him the audience which picked up on 'Purple Rain'. In the rest of the world, his following had stabilised at somewhere around the 1.3m mark. But sales tell only part of the picture. 'Sign' is ultimately a huge and satisfying masterclass in the modern pop, rock, soul, and r&b arts.

Sign 'O' The Times

The first single off the album, released in February, 1987 in the US (No 3) and March in the UK (No 8), had a peach and black sleeve featuring the singer's torso and legs (for once fully clothed) and Cat, her face hidden by a large heart. The heart motif recurs throughout the packaging adding to the use of letters and

figures as words, a sort of street symbology: U=you, 4=for, 2=to or too. It had been seeping into the album design from 'Controversy' onwards. Now, the 'O' in the title of 'Sign' is the Ban the Bomb insignia. It's also the decorative tag on the zip to his high-heeled boots.

Against a sparse, throbbing R&B track dominated by synthesised and 'real' percussion, Prince gives an unblinking overview of a troubled land. Perhaps it is because he's singing about a grim snapshot vision of America, but there is in the phrasing of his vocal an echo of Marvin Gaye. Imagine a family or friends sitting at the kitchen table, flicking through the morning paper, picking out the big stories and adding their personal anecdotes to illustrate the grim litany. There does not seem to be much hope. AIDs, gang wars, drug wars, the bomb (it's still before the Cold War thawed) and natural disasters. There is huge spending on Star Wars and the space shuttle but the desperate poverty trap in what is supposed to be the world's richest country remains. Let's fall in love, get married, have a baby, he sings. Call the baby Nate, presumably not short for Nathaniel but Nate as in Nativity, the birth of

Christ. The message is: We are in need of a Second Coming to sort out this mess.

Play In The Sunshine

After the gloom of 'Sign', the hope of its last thought is carried on by this rumbustious rock 'n' roller taken at full-pelt in celebration of a life filled with an energy that is not chemically assisted. The lyric is full of skittish imagery and vivid colour and, after the unequivocal no drugs, no alcohol stance of the first verse, could be open to a less certain interpretation. But the lasting drive is to bring prodigals back into the fold. Susannah Melvoin adds the background voice.

Housequake

In which Prince raps. The track, which was recorded for the 'Camille' album, is a Clintonesque mix of tight danceable funk, James Brown horn riffs and the Godfather's get down rap-as-vocal. On the 'Camille' album, the vocal track was speeded slightly to give it a girlish sound with the intention of 'selling' Camille as someone other than Prince. On this evidence, fat chance. As well as being a great funk charge and homage to the James Brown way of things funky, 'Housequake' is tremendous fun. He and the band certainly have a ball doing it on stage.

The Ballad Of Dorothy Parker

After his bow to Brown and Clinton, the vocal here gives a big nod to Sly Stoned funk. But the lyric is elliptical. It starts life as The Great American Short Story incarnate – a meeting between a waitress in a short order restaurant and the troubled customer. Like such meetings, however, it is a love that fails to reach fulfilment. As did Prince's attempted collaboration with Joni Mitchell, a long time favourite. So here he quoted her name and a line from one of her songs ('Help Me' from 'Court & Spark', 1974) in the narrative.

It

Like 'Sign', another sparse-sounding track driven by a drum machine but in a throwback to 'Controversy', the lyric is driven by the desire to have sex. He's a humpin' kind of a guy, who'll do it anywhere. Picture him, heavily-lidded and pouting, prowling the corridors of Paisley Park which echoes once again with the screaming sounds of berserk, rampant carnality.

Starfish And Coffee

Co-written by Susannah Melvoin, this is in mood and tone a refinement of his hippy-dippy psychedelic period. A sunny and thoroughly amiable track, it is simple and simply done with none of the kitchen-sink instrumentation which would have been used had he recorded it with The Revolution for 'Around The World' or 'Parade'. In this, 'Starfish' reveals why he needed to return to the basics of recording alone and take a step or two backwards to move several forward.

Slow Love

A ballad, co-written by Carol Davis, on whose 1989 debut 'Heart Of Gold' it would subsequently appear. Collaboration with women seems to have increasingly softened Prince's view on sex from being a battle for supremacy, a fight to the climax, to something which could be intercourse in the true sense of the word –

a communication between people, a sharing. Here is Exhibit A for the defence. A classic – as in adhering to a well-defined form – soul ballad arrangement, 'Slow Love' again has little embellishment, although Eric Leeds's sax threatens to run away with the song at one point, and all other assistance comes from women – Clare Fischer (string arrangement), Wendy (guitar, vocal) and Lisa (vocal). The transition from the lewd, leering, sneering priapic Prince of the early eighties to the adult pleasuring sex machine is complete. He'll remember this woman's name afterwards.

Hot Thing

An uncomplicated dance-funk paean to young flesh, 'Hot Thing' is notable for the use of a crisp, clipped horn riff from Leeds and Bliss and a more expansive solo. The pumping rhythm was made for Cat choreography.

Forever In My Life

Another spare, unvarnished rhythm track driven only by synths and drum/drum machines until the last 30 seconds. And, in tune with the stripped clean nature of the track, Prince

bares his soul. He wants to settle down for Heaven's sake! His singing has an impassioned, believable gospel feel and is one of his most mature and complete vocal performances. The twist in the tail: throughout one assumes that he is making these promises of uncomplicated loyalty to a woman. At the end, it is clear that it's also a prayer to God.

U Got The Look

The third single off the album, a duet between Prince as 'Camille' and Sheena Easton, for whom Prince, as Alexander Nevermind, had written and produced 'Sugar Walls' (1984). On drums and percussion, Sheila E thuds a four-square, heavily clomping hard rock beat. After the abject failure in the USA of the second single ('If I Was Your Girlfriend'), 'Look' reached No 2 there. In the UK it peaked at No 11. There are few less adventurous tracks on the album.

If I Was Your Girlfriend

Released as the second single off 'Sign', the intriguing concept implied by the lyric was clearly too much for the American public. It

reached only No 67 on the Hot 100. Sung with his voice slightly doctored as 'Camille', Prince wants to be all of the things to his girlfriend that she is to him. If that isn't love and devotion, what is? But as an investigation of his feminine side, it is not *too* shocking. He's simply taking upon himself a few tasks involved in being best friends. New Man in Rock is a slim volume so far and is likely to remain so but this track might provide the starting point for one of the early chapters. He pleads his cause to a gentle, slow-walkin' tempo which found more favour in the UK, where it got to No 13.

Strange Relationship

Taken from the proposed and shelved 'Camille' album, 'Strange Relationship' is a thumping, 4/4 pop-rock tune with a lyric that, like 'If I Was Your Girlfriend', is only too aware that love, as opposed to sex, is not the simplest of emotions. The narrator of 'Relationship' is the dissatisfied sort of man who can't bear to see his lover happy, because he isn't, but when he makes her unhappy he can't bear to see her sad. He can't live with her, can't live without her. In the real world, unless this man gets himself sorted out, the situation has all the ingredients for domestic violence. In the world of pop, it makes for a good album track and further evidence that Prince has knowledge of a broad range of human relationships.

I Could Never Take The Place Of Your Man

Does Prince just zip off these fizzy little numbers to show how easy he finds it to create white pop-rock? Of course, making it sound easy is often the mark of careful preparation, but here there is a real sense of bashing it out, getting it down quickly on tape so as not to lose the moment. With a chiming refrain, not unlike an instrumental hook fashioned by a revivalist pop-rocker like Marshall Crenshaw, and beaty trap drumming, it tells the tale of a pick-up in a club. She's a deserted mum, looking for affection, 'a good man' and a relationship. He, meanwhile, is on the look-out for a quickie. Very quick resolution to the title. It was released as the fourth single off the album by which time, incidentally, a film based on the 1987 'Sign' tour had been shot, in Europe and

at Paisley Park, edited and released to great acclaim in movie theatres in the USA. 'I Could Never Take The Place' reached No 10 in the States, No 29 in the UK.

The Cross

Having shown us how to construct, perform and produce simple pop rock songs, Prince's masterclass continued with this dark and impressive rock anthem. Power chords? Here's how it's done. Where 'Purple Rain' was all uplift, this is an awesome song about the redemption of human suffering by Christ. The lyric is simple. There is a better life to come. The guitar-based track which accompanies it grows from a tiny figure, through strong chording into a gradually rising storm of turbulent rock. This is rich, painterly rock, all dark washes of colour. The guitar work before the solid 4/4 tread of the drums comes in recalls that of Carlos Santana, one of his early models. But thereafter the piece turns up to full blast, and repeats, to build a fearful intensity with Prince singing harder than ever before.

It's Gonna Be A Beautiful Night

A fond farewell to The Revolution. Using a basic track recorded live at Le Zenith Club in Paris, France during the 1986 'Parade' tour and overdubbed prior to release, 'Beautiful Night' would have been better had it minimised even further the audience participation and hooting. (There is usually so much happening in Prince's performances in terms of musicianship and showmanship that he does not need the crutch of audience participation.) But, nonetheless, it's a vivacious example of the extra breadth the horn section has added to his music (Eric Leeds is co-writer with Prince and Matt Fink). Susannah Melvoin and Jill Jones add vocals, Sheila E steps in for percussion fills and a rap down the phone (Transmississippirap) and Miko Weaver fills on lead guitar. A great *band* performance.

Adore

The album ends with a piece of outstanding soul ballad singing. Prince's vocal on 'Adore' recalls, more than usually, other singers in the soul-gospel tradition who use falsetto or very high tenor register – Eddie Kendricks, Curtis Mayfield, Otis Leaville, Eugene Record of The Chi-Lites, William Hart of The Delfonics. Against a lovely, 'traditional' soul horn figure, Prince describes his devotion in as complete and helpless terms as he has ever uttered. But there is humour. Enumerating the sacrifices he'd make, he sings about his fine clothes (she could burn them), his car (she could smash it) – er, 'well maybe not the ride' he retracts quickly. 'Adore' brings to an end the best Prince album. And like the first three tracks of '1999', the final four tracks of 'Sign' comprise a magical, sustained piece of recording which marks him as unique among his generation as an alchemist of styles. He stays true to the roots of all the music while moulding it into a style and sound which is definably and demonstrably his own.

LOVESEXY

(FIRST RELEASED MAY 1988. PAISLEY PARK/WARNER BROS VINYL 25720-1, CD 25720-2.
UK VINYL WEA WX 164 AND WX 164CD.)

A little over a year after work began, the up-dated $10m Paisley Park studio complex opened for business on September 11, 1987. It's an impressive facility with three studios of varying sizes, one of which can be used for rehearsals or video shoots as well as recording. The sound stage is akin to a concert hall.

In the two months prior to the official opening, Prince had been recording music which would not be released officially until 1994, although it was one of the most sought-after bootlegs. Known as 'The Black Album', the tracks are dealt with at the later stage in the chronology of its official release. As Prince tells it, he had a kind of vision or revelation which gave him pause for serious thought about the content and direction of his music in general and of this record in particular.

Recording alone again, the songs had become progressively darker as time went on. In terms of his career, the manifestation has taken on the mantle of the Divine revelation of Saul on the road to Damascus, although the way he describes it has more than a touch of Hieronymous Bosch mixed in with Walt Disney's vision in *Fantasia* of Modest Mussorgsky's 'A Night On Bare Mountain'. It was 'a dark night of the soul when a lot of things happened in a few hours'. And so 'The Black Album' was pulled on 1 December, 1987, a week before release.

As his own riposte to this dark, angry side, he cut 'Lovesexy' with the basic Sign 'O' The Times band in seven weeks in December, 1987 and January, 1988 mostly in the order in which it appeared on the record. He described 'Lovesexy' as a state of mind which he had reached and there is indeed a sense of spiritual energy and regeneration at the heart of much of the album, intertwined with the usual imperatives of the flesh. With this self-knowledge, he asserted, 'you know who you are, and what your name is' and, as we were to learn a few years down the line, his name was not in fact Prince. He had also decided to be more leisurely about his approach to life and work, which history has shown us was, and is, virtually impossible and utterly foreign to him.

On 'Lovesexy', his 10th album, individual members of his then current band, particularly Boni Boyer's voice, Sheila E and the Eric Leeds/Atlanta Bliss horn section were featured.

With tracks segueing one into the next and a lighter, more positive atmosphere created by the generally upbeat songs, the record is shot through with news of a quest for spiritual salvation and an affirmation of faith and belief. It is ambitious, but not a success. It's good moments – a catchy pop hit and a ballad – are as good as most of his best work in those styles. But overall the complexity of the arrangement too often confuses and dims the melodies.

The album's sleeve design was as controversial as that for 'Dirty Mind' but Prince was rather better known now and the fuss created was consequently greater. Aside from a gold chain and pendant, he is naked and perched on a blow-up of one of the more lewd flower blooms in the grand botanical scheme. His right hand rests on his heart – a gesture that says simply and emphatically that this is personal and this is the truth. Just by his right bicep, the stamen of the flower rises up, pointing tumescently at him. This did not go down well in 1988 America. Many radio stations and the printed media reviewed the album sleeve, not the album. Several record store chains refused to stock the album, others stocked it but would not display, keeping it under the shelf like a pornographic magazine. Bearing in mind that this is one of his least lubricious recordings, it was irony in the extreme.

With moderate exposure at best, the album sold poorly in the USA reaching No 11 on the album charts, sales barely scraping past the million mark. In Europe, by contrast, his star continued in the ascendant. 'Lovesexy' sold over a million-and-a-half and went to No 1 in the UK and on several other continental charts.

'Either you went with it and had a mind-blowing experience or you didn't,' he said. Of all his albums, it is perhaps the most enigmatic, which is saying something. To ensure that the message would not be mistaken, spiritual rebirth was the central theme of the 'Lovesexy' tour that followed.

I No

The first track is prefaced by Ingrid Chavez, a poet Prince met in a Minneapolis club in 1987. Credited as 'Spirit Child', she recites a brief verse against wispy New Age sounds: 'Rain is wet/And sugar is sweet/Clap your hands/And stomp you feet/Everybody knows when love calls/You gotta go'. Prince then introduces The New Power Generation, a title he would later officially attach to his band.

More symbology. On the album sleeve and throughout the lyric, I is shown as a crude drawing of an eye. The lyric makes play on the identical sound, though not spelling or meaning, between no and know. So whenever we see the drawing of an eye and 'no' we read 'I know'.

'I No', first recorded as 'The Ball' for the 'Crystal Ball' album of 1986, is a tight funk track showing the band off to excellent effect. They're all working busily around Prince as he rather rushes through the telling of his revela-

tion during the recording of 'The Black Album'.

There is talk about peer pressure to take drugs, drink, use a gun – the anti-drug crusade's slogan 'Just Say No' gets frequent reaffirmation – but the most noticeable message is one that is a very traditional black gospel theme. The devil talks in a loud voice; the Lord calls to you softly. Who you gonna hear?

Alphabet St.

Reached via a babble of chattering tongues (which were on the end of the 1986 recording of 'The Ball') and a final, 'No!' at the end of 'I No', 'Alphabet St.' is the album's most accessible uptempo sound and not surprisingly was selected as the first single, released in April, 1987. It reached No 10 in the US, No 11 in the UK.

Based on a solid rock/R&B riff with poppin' bass courtesy of Levi Seacer and vocal decorations – a 'yeah, yeah, yeah' vocal from The Beatles' phrasebook, his 'gotta, gotta' sounds like Otis Redding, for instance – the song comes in two parts. The skittish feel of the early verses in which he describes how he'd

like to pick up a girl in a white Thunderbird and drive her to Tennessee. At the end of the second verse, the horns enter, the musical stakes increase and the lyric states the real purpose of 'Alphabet St.': 'Put the right letters together and make a better day'.

In part two, Cat Glover struts on to rap and the rock is buried utterly under Sheila E's funky syncopated drumming, chicken-scratch guitar and the band's enthusiastic vamping on the groove. It's doubtful whether discord, such as is used by the band's horn section and keyboards, has ever been played to quite such good effect on a hit single before or since.

Glam Slam

A determinedly pop-rock approach with Beatles-like harmonies, a depth of sound reminiscent of John Lennon's 'I Am The Walrus' and a wallop to the drums as though Phil Spector was calling the shots. 'The glam of them all' was a phrase in 'Alphabet St.' and here the 'glam slam' is a love that KOs with one punch, satisfies with one touch. It attempts to explain the intensity of a physical

love in less visceral language than he has hitherto used.

Released as the second single, it stiffed completely in the USA not even making the Top 100. In the UK the single reached No 29 (he was on tour in Europe). The adhesive pop chorus was just a little too cute for the late 80s.

Anna Stesia

Superficially a plaintively pretty song about loneliness, Prince soon extends the theme from personal loneliness via some vivid lines on the gnawing hunger for physical contact to ultimate fulfilment through spiritual oneness with God. This is an almost exact description of his sudden discovery of his true 'self'. The song ends with a promise to dedicate himself to spreading the word – 'I'll tell Your story'.

The multi-tracked voices and increasingly edgy accompaniment are not entirely compatible with a state of grace he has found. An effective ballad, though.

Dance On

On vinyl, this track started side two and with the final track bookended the music with slabs of real life portraiture. Every so often, his output tells us, Prince gets obsessed by the stream of violence on the TV news. 'Small' wars, gang wars, the ever-present threat of a nuclear catastrophe, muggings, random killings. His solution to end the rampant mayhem is to educate the children, sweep away the status quo. Unimpeachable motives, but much of the sloganising doesn't stand up to analysis. The music, on the other hand, is muscular and pumped up on steroids from the moment Sheila E clatters round the kit, parks it on the snare drum and ushers in Levi Seacer's bass.

Lovesexy

A big, thumping production that tries to take on the mantle of '1999' but doesn't really work. Where similar tracks sound full of body, this is merely cluttered and unfocused, like several of the over-reaching arrangements on the album. On the lyric sheet, he prefaces the song with the comment that 'Lovesexy' is the feeling of falling in love with the heavens above, not with an earthling boy or girl. This is not the impression the song gives and it remains one of his weakest title tracks.

When 2 R In Love

With 'Alphabet St.' the highlight of the album and the only track from 'The Black Album' saved for 'Lovesexy'. A ballad with a delicious, creamy melody, beautifully sung in falsetto, against a rich pattern of sound, all cushions and silks. When two are in love nothing is taboo.

I Wish U Heaven

A loud, smacking drum machine and bass throb drive a pop melody. The comparatively brief track sounds a trifle unfinished compared to the over-wrought songs elsewhere on the album. It was the third single off the album and, like 'Glam Slam', did not make the US charts. In the UK it reached No 24.

Positivity

If not entirely a summing up of the album's basic messages, the mid-tempo funk of 'Positivity' unquestionably attempts to capture the essence of Prince's moral redefinition. So, we get a list of questions addressed to youth about crime because these are the hope for the future. So far, so lucid if predictable. Then he refers back to his run in with the devil – 'Spooky Electric', the dark side entity who appeared at the very beginning of 'I No'. This is the dark side against which we must all fight.

BATMAN: Motion Picture Soundtrack

(FIRST RELEASE JUNE 1989 US WARNER BROS 25936-1, CD 25936-2.
UK VINYL WEA WX 281, CD WEA 925936-2)

Although it still seems as unlikely as heavy snow in August, the plan, after the Lovesexy tour, was for rest and studio work on other projects. The tour, with its first half comprising medleys of the older, explicit material about desire, lust and copulation in its manifold varieties and the second part explaining his Divine revelation and subsequent spiritual awakening, was an exhausting trek. It was, he said, like reliving the revelation every night.

But during a break in the tour, his management urged him to consider the overtures the Warner Bros film division had been making to them for Prince to contribute to a soundtrack. *Batman* was to be the first big budget project of director Tim Burton after considerable success with smaller-budget films – *Pee-Wee's Big Adventure* and *Beetlejuice*. It transpired that Burton and one of his stars, Jack Nicholson, who was cast as The Joker in the adaptation of the comic characters for the big screen, were Prince fans. Two songs, '1999' and 'Baby, I'm A Star', had been used on the soundtrack of the film's rough cut and created the atmosphere needed by the director.

He took some persuading – but there were very persuasive reasons for him to do the project. First, his most commercial album to date had been one of songs from the soundtrack to his own film. Second, in the USA his sales of his albums had been falling steadily. 'Lovesexy' sold more outside the States than in it. Third, *Batman* was a big budget movie, with all the advantages of a huge and very high-profile promotion push prior to its premiere. Fourth, although he had excellent revenue from Controversy Music, his publishing firm, there were music industry rumours that he was in some financial difficulty because of a combination of falling record sales, tours that were sold out but costly to mount, an expensive, newly-opened studio complex to run and a Paisley Park label that had no hits. Fifth, for a DIY writer-producer-performer of Prince's talents a soundtrack album was a *comparatively* easy undertaking because all he needed to do was read a screenplay, watch the rushes and write music based on what he read and, mostly, saw and didn't everyone already know the basics of *Batman* anyhow? Sixth, he could probably use up some of the dozens of tracks left over from other or aborted projects which he had secreted in the Paisley Park vaults, racks of the stuff already recorded which would fit in very nicely. Seventh, he would get paid a lot for it. Eighth, the battle between good and evil, which Burton's initially more interesting examination of the psychology of the Batman character focused on, was one with which Prince could closely identify given his recent epiphany, album and tour.

He began writing and recording material for the soundtrack in December, 1988 and, with a break for the final Japanese leg of the Lovesexy tour, continued through January, 1989 and part of February. At the same time, he restructured the team of advisers who had been with him since before the success of 'Purple Rain'.

First, he replaced his Press representatives, the Howard Bloom Organisation. Next, he parted company with his management at

Cavallo, Ruffalo & Fargnoli, and replaced them with Albert Magnoli, who they had introduced to Prince as director of 'Purple Rain'. Magnoli in turn hired the legal firm which included ace music business lawyer John Branca, the man who brokered Stevie Wonder's deals with Motown, to replace Prince's long-time legal adviser Lee Phillips. (Magnoli scarcely lasted a year as manager – a disagreement over Prince's next project, the *Graffiti Bridge* movie, severed the arrangement before the end of 1989.)

After the collaborative effort of 'Lovesexy', Prince returned to a one-man operation at the Paisley Park studio for 'Batman' with minor contributions from his horn section and Clare Fischer's Orchestra. On one of the songs which corresponds to scenes between Batman/Bruce Wayne and Vicki Vale, Sheena Easton sang the female vocal. She also co-wrote it. He shares writing credit on one other track with John L Nelson, his father. The Minneapolis gospel choir The Sounds of Blackness also added vocals to one track.

Prince is not too constrained by the demands of the soundtrack format and actually uses the dramatic thrust of the story to link the songs and give the album impetus. He sings in the guise of Batman, The Joker, Bruce Wayne and Vicki Vale and uses snippets of dialogue from the movie to spice the tracks or provide quirky introductions.

'Batman' was commercially his most successful album since 'Purple Rain' and first No 1 since 'Around The World In A Day'. It sold a million in its first week, six million worldwide. Not as staggering as the film, which grossed $40m in its first weekend, but a useful enough commercial enterprise.

The Future

Prince sings as Batman. The voice of Michael Keaton, who plays the character in the film, whispers huskily to a miscreant, 'I want you to tell all your friends about me' and we glide smoothly into a solid, flowing 4/4 dance track. He's seen the future and it's – a dancefloor! Well, not quite. The vision of the future on earth is bleak – drugs, guns, poverty – so the new world 'needs spirituality that will last'. (The *Batman* soundtrack becomes a continuation of his 'Lovesexy' message.) It's an effec-

tinctive exhortation to 'Think about the future!' bridging the two tracks. A straight, hard, rock-funk track heavy on the drums, power chords and screaming solos. If impure thoughts are a crime, he sings across the dancefloor, he's not just guilty, he's worthy of the electric chair.

The Arms of Orion

Co-written with Sheena Easton and sung as a duet between Vicki Vale and Bruce Wayne, this piece is a wearily typical soundtrack ballad, one of the few songs on the album that sounds as if it could come from any movie or, indeed, from any writer/singer. The third single off 'Batman', it reached No 32 (US) and No 27 (UK).

Partyman

'Gentlemen! Let's broaden our minds,' says Jack Nicholson as The Joker, inviting his pack to ransack an art gallery. We are back in firmer funk-dance territory. The music is standard fare, nothing exceptional, and had been in the Prince vaults for some considerable time. The lyrics are dictated by the character's burning desire to destroy the status quo by creating

tive opening cut, grim lyrics and music again using dissonance to create an atmosphere of foreboding, but holding out the offer of hope. Although a line like 'Systematic overthrow of the underclass' might have seemed pleasing because of the over/under interplay, the sociopolitical logic of it is somewhat awry – how can a powerless underclass be overthrown?

Electric Chair

Sung as The Joker with Jack Nicholson's dis-

anarchy and then replace it with his own despotic rule. 'Partyman' was the second single off the album and reached No 18 in the USA and No 14 in the UK.

Vicki's Waiting

'I'm of a mind to make some mookie,' chuckles The Joker, before this undemanding midtempo light funk song, sung by Prince as Bruce Wayne, trundles in. It was one of the first songs recorded for the soundtrack and was easy to do, one assumes, because everyone who has ever read – or merely read about – the comics knows that Bruce loves Vicki, Vicki loves Batman and here is the conundrum:– when does he reveal his true identity? While he is making up his mind he tells her a coarse joke about the respective dimensions of a man's penis and a woman's vagina. 'Vicki didn't laugh at all,' he sings. What a surprise.

Trust

Partyup time as The Joker feeds the greed of Gotham City residents by showering them with greenbacks. The groove is fast, furious and funky and makes for one of the more

effective tracks on the album because of its sheer simplicity. Prince allows himself the final word: 'Who do ya trust if U can't trust God?' Shining with all the goodness of 'Lovesexy', he answers his own question. 'Nobody.'

Lemon Crush

Vicki Vale's song. A full production, with percussive keyboards and drum machines elbowing for space in a funky, uptempo groove which dislocates in the final quarter. Quite an effective notion this for Ms Vale is attracted and perplexed by the quality of mouth-to-mouth she's getting. Like the majority of the up-tempo tracks on 'Batman', 'Lemon Crush' almost works but one can't help feeling that were this the 'real' follow up to 'Lovesexy' and not something customised for a movie it would have been set aside and worked on later, put on a B-side or given to another Paisley Park act.

Scandalous

A ballad co-written with Prince's father, 'Scandalous' is sung falsetto by Batman. The lyric of hot sex and fantasy fulfilment is set against disquietingly dissonant sweeps of keyboards. Compared to his best ballads, from 'Do Me Baby' through 'When 2 R In Love', 'Scandalous' is small potatoes. It was released in the United States as a single. Didn't make the pop list but got to No 5 in the black chart. It was not released as a single in the UK.

Batdance

The grand finale. All of the film's characters, major and minor, take a speaking, singing or sampled role in what amounts to a potted version of the plot and thumbnail sketch of the main protagonists and their philosophies. Prince's recent all-encompassing absorption with the battle between good and evil seems to have given him an empathy with the villain, The Joker, whose sampled voice is a catalyst to each twist in the track, the link between its sections. (Of course, it is quite possible that he realised he had no choice because Jack Nicholson's character had all the best lines and his performance stole the movie.)

A splash of loud rock guitar and The Joker's sarcastic aside – 'Oh, I got a live one here!' –

kick open the door to let in a locomotion of keyboards driving the first section with the choir's chant of 'Bat-maaan' referring directly back to the theme from the original TV series. Then drums settle the beat into a straight, driving 4/4 rocker which gets funkier as Prince grooves on Hammond organ.

The Joker's next interruption, 'And where is the Batman?' is the cue for a loud rock guitar solo to muscle in. It shuts down as suddenly as it started when the Joker purrs 'Stop the Press, who is that?' and switching to tight mid tempo funk at walking pace. Vicki Vale sashays by to the accompaniment of scratched guitar chords. Bruce Wayne introduces himself.

Finally, prefaced by The Joker/Nicholson's assertion that 'This town needs an enema!' there's a brief up-tempo 4/4 dance, the highlight of which is Prince's close meshing of rhythm guitars. As a whole, the track is deliberately disjointed, a clever and interesting use of samples, and a must for Jack Nicholson fans.

The lack of logical flow, let alone a cohesive feel or a simple rhythm, made 'Batdance' an unlikely single release. But it was his sixth US No 1 and reached No 2 in the UK.

GRAFFITI BRIDGE

(FIRST RELEASED AUGUST, 1990 US PAISLEY PARK/WARNER BROS VINYL 27493-1, CD 27493-2;
UK VINYL WEA WX 361, CD 759927493-2.)

'Batman' was a rare instance in Prince's career in which he had been forced into more sub-
servient role. Although he wrote, performed and produced the music on the album almost
entirely alone, his contribution to the finished movie turned out to be no more than a cypher
in the equation. And even on the record, a line or two of Jack Nicholson dialogue stole the
tracks as surely as a look or a sentence hi-jacked every scene in which he appeared. But the
album put Prince back at the top of the charts. Indeed, film had never really let him down.
Purple Rain – big smash; *Cherry Moon* – awful film but 'Parade' got to No 3 in the USA; *'Sign
'O' The Times'* – acclaimed as one of the best concert movies ever. Then came *Batman.*

His next project was another soundtrack, a
double album of 'Music from Graffiti Bridge',
his third feature movie. But, unlike 'Batman', it
was not another solo showcase. In fact he
sang lead on only eight of the 17 tracks on
'Graffiti Bridge' and duetted on another two.
The Time feature heavily and Grand Wazir of
funk George Clinton, the majestic gospel
singer Mavis Staples, lead voice on the
Staples Singers' Stax Records hits in the sixties and seventies, and young Tevin Campbell,
barely out of his teens and a rising star after
working on Quincy Jones's 'Back On The
Block' album, all sang leads.

Some of the tracks or song ideas were tak-
en from unfinished projects or had been omitted from albums which had changed course
radically during recording. His bassist,
Levi Seacer Jr, became an increasingly
close collaborator at this time and is credited
as co-writer, producer and arranger on
several tracks.

Recording began in the summer of 1989
and lasted until January 1990, the movie was
then filmed and when that was wrapped he put
the finishing touches to the Nude tour, so
named for its lack of musical, not sartorial,
adornment. It was Back to Basics before the
phrase became a political slogan.

For 'Graffiti Bridge', Prince returned to

'Purple Rain' terrain, safe home territory or so he thought. Battle was resumed between The Kid and Morris Day, another scene-stealer, and on this occasion the future policy at a club, the Glam Slam, was the Big Deal at issue. The Kid favoured music with a message and Day wanted to sex it up. The band put together for the film included Seacer (bass), Miko Weaver (guitar), new drummer Michael Bland from Dr Mambo's Combo, three rapper/dancers Damon Dickson, Kirk Johnson and Tony Mosley, who went under the name of Game Boyz, and singer Rosie Gaines. She had cut an album, 'Caring', for Epic five years earlier. Levi Seacer had been the guitarist.

The script went through several versions – Madonna was mooted as leading lady, then Kim Basinger, who had played Vicki Vale in *Batman* (she and Prince had a relationship). When Basinger quit, the next rewrite had Ingrid Chavez in the role. Many cast members – Staples, Clinton and Campbell, Jill Jones, Robin Power, a new addition to the Paisley Park team, and T C Ellis – had little or no pretension to great acting ability.

The film cost $10m and was shot at Paisley Park in a little over a month. Previews in Pasadena – box office business there for *Purple Rain* had been the best anywhere in the US – were as bad as they could be and re-edits in June and July did not get much of a response from the company.

While remedial work went on, Prince did the European leg of the Nude tour which was, as good as his word, stripped down in terms of music and presentation. The band was essentially the film line-up plus Matt Fink, who had stayed away from the movie set to programme the synthesisers for the tour. Lucky him.

The 'Music from Graffiti Bridge' album came out as scheduled in August. The film was late, following three months later in November. 'I see this more like those 1950s rock and roll movies,' Prince told *Rolling Stone*. The critics saw it more like a turkey and panned it almost without exception. The paying public endorsed this view at the box office.

Graffiti Bridge was essentially a collection of music videos dangling on a thin line of plot sustained by a script that was far too naïve for the nineties and buried by acting that was every bit as amateurish as a glance at its cast list suggested it would be. A movie is not just a set of images that are good to look at. Narrative drive and believable characterisation are thought to be an advantage too. As usual, Morris Day and Jerome Benton are scene-stealers, but that is not saying a great deal in the context of this particular film.

The album did not do particularly well either, selling a little over a million in the USA where it reached No 6. But it's by no means his worst, has some good tight funk and tough dance grooves, though it lacks the hit melody or three. The album artwork, too, might have reminded those with long memories of Prince's deeply uneven 'Around The World In A Day' LP. (Iconologists will have noted that the design blending the male and female symbols which will reach its evolved stage with the 'Symbol' album is almost complete. It appears as an earring and as the 't' in 'Graffiti'.)

Can't Stop This Feeling I Got

'Dear Dad,' he whispers, 'things didn't turn out quite like I wanted them to. Sometimes I feel like I'm gonna explode'. A very low-key introduction to the feeling he got which is fizzily optimistic. Performed entirely by Prince as a guitar-bass-drums combo with very discreet piano and keyboard fills, 'Can't Stop' had been recorded in 1986 but a new version was laid down for the soundtrack. A pop-rock bop.

New Power Generation

The third single off the album, it reached No 64 in the US (UK, No 26). A funky 4/4 with, unusually, the fabulously fatback drumming credited to Morris Day. The refrain 'Lay down your funky weapon/Come join us on the floor/Making love and music's/The only thing worth fighting for' owes something in ideology and tactics to the manifesto George Clinton had been propounding since the early seventies. The New Power Generation, no longer very amused at being told what to do, is here to sweep away old fashioned music and ideas. (After the Nude tour there would be further

alterations to the personnel of Prince's road band and it would take the name New Power Generation.)

Release It

A track by The Time driven by busily funky drumming which sets up Morris Day as the slick, super-confident nasty boy of the film. Written by Prince with Levi Seacer, who also shares producer and arranger credit, the energy is reminiscent of 'Housequake'. Saxophonist Candy Dulfer adds a few riffs on the fade but it is a peripheral contribution. The track, like all of The Time's contributions to *Graffiti Bridge*, was recorded for 'Corporate World', an album project started in June, 1989 but interrupted when *Graffiti Bridge* went into pre-production. The Time album that eventually came out a year later was named, very aptly, 'Pandemonium'.

The Question of U

All his own work, this is what a standard slow, blues becomes in the hands of Prince. The 'U' he is asking the questions of is himself. More impressive than the lyric or singing is the very fine guitar solo, which has the logic and phrasing of a passage by Carlos Santana, one of his more obvious and acknowledged influences.

Elephants & Flowers

All his own work, again, and recorded at the time of 'Batman', 'Elephants' argues the case of a good man trying to find his way in a hard town. Its groove is not unlike a brusquer rock mutation of 'Alphabet St.' 'There will be peace for those who love God a lot,' is the repeated resolution. In spite of its apparent importance to the thrust of the story and motivation of the character, it's a filler.

Round And Round

Sung by Tevin Campbell to a track otherwise entirely concocted by Prince, this is how the once-mooted collaboration between Prince and Michael Jackson might have sounded. The weedy sound of the drum machines and synthesised bass parts make for an extraordinarily thin sounding track. 'Round And Round' was the second single off the album and reached No 12 in the US.

We Can Funk

Not in the strict sense a duet with Parliafunkadlicment leader George Clinton, more a shared lead vocal. A democratic sound in other ways too. The chorus is pure Clinton, and most of the background vocal arrangement veers towards his style, as does the line 'We bin funkin' over here, over there ain't shit'. But the keyboard decorations are straight out of the Prince hookbook. They shared the writing credit too and it bristles with small references to the work of each. The song had first been recorded in 1986, was re-cut with the Eric Leeds/Atlanta Bliss horn section and vocal back-up from Gary Shider, a Funkadelic guitarist, Tracey Lewis, Belita Woods, Joseph Fiddler, Steve Boyd, William Payne, Sandra Dance, Mike Harris and Pat Lewis.

Joy In Repetition

All his own work from the 1986 'Crystal Ball' sessions, it was scheduled to follow 'The Ball' and uses a segue originally cut to link the tracks. For once the lyric at least describes the action a tad.

Love Machine

A Time track with lead vocal by Morris Day and Elisa Fiorillo, who sounds not unlike one of the less talented Jackson sisters. Appropriated from the 'Corporate World' sessions, the highlight is a fast seduction conversation between Day and Fiorillo. Writing credits were shared by Prince and Levi Seacer 'with Morris Day' which presumably means he wrote his own part, which pretty much consisted of ad-libbed asides to the girl's lead vocal. Seacer is also credited with assists in production and arrangement.

Tick, Tick, Bang

Written for Vanity 6 in the early eighties, a do-it-all Prince is being teased to distraction, or more precisely to premature ejaculation. There's a lot happening in the track to very little effect.

Shake!

An R&B dance cut by The Time. Terse, tight, not to say uptight, jerky and shot through with subtle references to fifties and sixties soul and R&B music, such as a great guitar figure that Steve Cropper might properly call his own and a Sam The Sham keyboard refrain that has the feel and sound of 'Woolly Bully' if not the notation. It was released as the album's fifth single.

Thieves In The Temple

The first single off 'Graffiti Bridge', a No 6 US hit and No 7 UK hit. How optimistic this must have made the parties involved feel about the prospects for both album and film. The star recorded it alone again but aside from the chorus there's little to distinguish it as prime Prince. In the light of its commercial success it seems odd that the far more effective 'Can't Stop', which opened the album, was never released as a single.

The Latest Fashion

The final Time contribution to the album was from 'Corporate World' but substantially remodelled by using the melody from another Time track. Prince joins the band who take co-production and arranging credits. They hit a typically jabbing funk groove, Candy Dulfer blows a sax solo, there's plenty of exhortation to-and-froing between members of the band.

PRINCE : GRAFFITI BRIDGE

Melody Cool

Amen. Mavis Staples, who by now had released 'Time Waits For No One' on Paisley Park, sings the socks off a Prince tune clearly written to recall the Staples Singers in their pomp. The Steeles' vocal background substituted for Mavis's father, brother and sister. The performance is better than the song, which is not helped by the weedy, wooden drum sound.

Still Would Stand All Time

Following the plot of the movie – The Kid battling with Day for control of the club, The Kid losing his guardian angel (she really *is* an angel) but realising that the salvation is within himself, he is still deep in Lovesexy divinity mode – this ballad was written prior to the Lovesexy tour. The Steeles gospel group gives the vocal a sanctified depth. With his usual thoroughness, Prince has the vocal preaching and testifying moves down to the last gasp and grunt. Whether his voice has the depth, weight and gravitas to truly achieve what it attempts here is another matter.

Graffiti Bridge

As with the album's first song it is hard to understand why this Big Production number – Clare Fischer Orchestra makes its one contribution – was not released as a single. It has a simple, swaying rhythm, a catchy chorus, an instrumental hook that seems to have fallen off a Christmas carol, and a feeling of quiet, steadfast hope that there is a happy land at the end of every search. Levi Seacer (bass), Boni Boyer (organ), Sheila E (drums) all sing background and Mavis Staples and Tevin Campbell are featured.

New Power Generation (Pt II)

A final thumping reprise of NPG with extra vocals from Mavis Staples, Tevin Campbell, Robin Power and a rap by T C Ellis. And as the water laps under Graffiti Bridge the filtered voice intones; 'The New Power Generation has just taken control'.

PRINCE
& THE NEW
POWER
GENERATION
DIAMONDS AND PEARLS

DIAMONDS AND PEARLS

(FIRST RELEASED OCTOBER, 1991. US PAISLEY PARK/WARNER BROS CD 25379-2,
UK VINYL WX 432, CD 7599253379-2.)

After the Nude tour, which ended in September, 1990, Prince's band underwent one of its periodic personnel-quakes and was renamed officially as the New Power Generation. His very long-time keyboard man, Dr Fink, who had been with Prince virtually since the beginning of his Warner Bros recording career, finally left to concentrate on solo projects and production. Guitarist Miko Weaver left for the same reason.

They were replaced by Levi Seacer Jr, an increasingly important contributor to Prince's Paisley Park projects who now moved from bass to guitar, and by Tommy Elm, who was given the surname Barbarella after the Roger Vadim sci-fi comic-strip of a film which starred Jane Fonda and was much admired by Prince. Sonny Thompson, a seasoned Minneapolis bassist who had almost got the job in Prince's band when Andre Cymone left in 1981, replaced Seacer and was henceforth called Sonny T.

Rosie Gaines (keyboard, vocals), Michael Bland (drums) and the Game Boyz – Damon Dickson, Kirk Johnson and Tony Mosley – stayed on although the trio had more clearly defined roles. Dickson was primarily a dancer, Johnson's duties were spread between dancer, DJ and percussionist while Mosley, now known as Tony M, took on a much higher profile role as master of ceremonies and rapper.

Speaking of profiles, Prince's one as an artist was now well-defined. As a live performer, he had few if any equals. He put together excellent shows, each tour was fundamentally different to the previous in tone – first challenging, then sheer exuberance, next a spiritually inspired show, then stripped-to-the-bone music. He had abandoned the set list of songs for each date and was playing it much more off the cuff, more in keeping with the spontaneity of his informal, post-concert jams at clubs which went on into the wee small hours, sessions like the great jazz musicians of thirties, forties and fifties were wont to play.

But record sales were disappointing in the USA. His previous American No 1 single, 'Batman', was achieved on the back of a huge media campaign and interest in a multi-million dollar movie. Left to its own devices, his music appealed to a much narrower core of fans somewhere around the million mark. For an artist of such stature, this was disappointing. In fact, he'd never had a number one pop single that had *not* been featured in a film. His three other No 1 hits were 'When Doves Cry' and 'Let's Go Crazy' from 'Purple Rain' and 'Kiss' from 'Under The Cherry Moon', though I doubt that the latter can claim the credit for the sale of anything more than an extra bag or two of popcorn. Remarkably, excellent albums like '1999' and 'Sign 'O' The Times' did not have the juice to push a single to No 1.

He spent a lot of time on 'Diamonds And Pearls', the next studio album. The Nude tour ended in Japan in September, 1990 and less than a month later he was recording with the New Power Generation. They are credited *en masse* as participating in the composition, production, arrangement and performance of the tracks. The sessions went on throughout

the winter at studios in Los Angeles, Tokyo and London as well as Paisley Park and he finished in February, 1991. He also recorded tracks for a Game Boyz rap album, for the group Louie Louie, for Paula Abdul and for Martika's album 'Martika's Kitchen'. Busy boy, as ever.

And he decided to assume management of his own career. This meant arguing for prompt release of recorded material. One of the reasons why Prince has such a huge catalogue of unreleased tracks is his abundant productiveness. As Alan Leeds, his tour manager and Paisley Park vice-president until 1992, observed in the notes to 'The Hits', Prince's music is 'by and large written and performed for the moment' and 'should be available while it's relevant'.

He also promoted 'Diamonds And Pearls' much more vigorously in the US than before, playing at various music business events like disc jockey conventions and gatherings of wholesalers and so on, and putting out limited edition teaser tracks with bonus cuts.

When after several postponements 'Diamonds And Pearls' finally hit the stores the 13-song package was clearly an attempt at reclaiming a place on the pop charts to match his reputation. More accessible melodies and crisper arrangements in a variety of strong styles were its foundations. There's a 'live band' sound and feeling with the contributions of Rosie Gaines' vocals and Tony M's raps particularly prominent.

At over two million copies sold it doubled his sales in the USA, went to No 1 on the album charts and spawned four Top 30 pop hits, the first Prince album to do so since 1984's 'Purple Rain'. The album went to No 3 in the UK and sold three million in territories outside the USA.

Thunder

Love, a revelation of God and the power of Mother Nature elbow for attention as Prince plays all of the instruments – there's an astonishing array of musical colours – and multitracks layers of vocals. It might have been written in Los Angeles the morning after a Californian earthquake, in Minneapolis after Minnesota hurricane, or anywhere after a night of sexual temptation or one full of unsettling dreams of spiritual battle, revelation and salvation. The chorus, which gives the dizzyingly full track its solid underpinning, keeps the focus on the voice. In the UK 'Thunder' was released in a limited edition picture disc format and still got to No 30. This speaks in equal measure about the core of loyal fans in the UK and the mordant state of the British pop charts.

Daddy Pop

Arranged in the traditional soul band format of Sly & The Family Stone and Larry Graham's Graham Central Station, this excellent pop-funk groove is driven by tight Michael Bland drumming and furious Sonny T bass as the focus moves from voice to rhythm. Daddy Pop, of course, is Prince. He has a dig at his critics, admits he's got 'grooves and grooves up on the shelf/Deep purple concord jams', and makes a joke about his elusiveness and inaccessibility.

Diamonds And Pearls

After focusing first on the voice and second on rhythm in the two previous tracks, the spotlight now switches again to melody. The title track is a devotional love song, celebrating love and the hope it holds out. The very pretty tune is lifted by Rosie Gaines' superb soaring vocal which counterpoints Prince's gentler, 'straighter' reading. He said that he would never sing the pop ballad with anyone but Gaines. It was released as the fourth US single and reached No 3. In the UK it was the third single and got to No 25.

Cream

Reputedly written after staring at himself in the mirror – 'u're filthy cute and baby u know it' – 'Cream' is lyrically a much simpler expression of the idea of self-belief and self-confidence than he might have written. 'Cream' rises to the top, take that chance and so will you runs the logic. But he sings it *dirty* and the tiny guitar figures with which he laces together the lines are insinuating and suggestive. The rhymes, too, are a lot simpler: fire/desire, top/cop, dance/chance, stronger/longer. A

tight little pop-rock groove, it was the second single off the album and went to No 1 in the US, his fifth chart-topper there but the first one not in some way associated with a feature-length movie. In the UK it reached 15.

Strollin'

A cute pop songs that *swings*. Reminiscent of Smokey Robinson at his most skittish – though I doubt that his lyrics have ever suggested buying dirty magazines – Prince sings in a warm and gentle falsetto. With all the hate in the world, he sings, 'least we could do is make a joyful sound'.

Willing And Able

A fine example of his ability to mix, or to suggest a mixture of, styles. Michael Bland's four-on-the-floor bass drum gives the opening a reggae feel, the frisky guitar chording is southern African while the vocal track comes from way over there in the Amen Corner with a big gospel feel from the Steeles vocal group and the wailing Hammond organ. It was co-written with Seacer and Tony M.

Gett Off

A late addition to the package replacing 'Horny Pony', which was its B-side as a cassette single and limited edition 7". It peaked at No 21 in the US. In the UK it reached No 4. 'Gett Off' is a return to raunch, very heavy funk. He sings lowdown-and-dirty with solid, snapping snare drum and a bass with big bottom. Eric Leeds' flute is an unexpected house guest on the track. Compared to the sexual bragging of gangsta rap and ragga current at the time, it was an unthreatening invitation to pleasure though no less sure of itself – '23 positions in a one-night stand' does not refer to an evening spent rearranging the furniture though he does suggest sex in every room in the house.

Walk, Don't Walk

Pop and funk take a stroll together at walking pace and talk about staying true to your own self. Be steadfast and confident, positive and proud. And watch out for those cars honking in perfect syncopation. A piece of fluff with a message.

Jughead

A rap song co-written by Tony M and Kirk Johnson that got Prince into a tad of trouble. Former manager Steve Fargnoli thought that the rap at the end of the song, in which Tony M gives an assessment of managers as a form of life at least as low as politicians and tabloid journalists, was a direct attack on him and sued. They settled out of court, so who knows? Certainly the sentences about managers receiving monies on an artist's songs recorded during their relationship long after that relationship had finished bore a resemblance to an award won by Cavallo, Ruffalo & Fargnoli as part of their claim against Prince after he severed connections at the start of 1989.

Money Don't Matter 2 Night

The feel of the instrumental track and vocal background as well as the humane message of the song has much in common with Stevie Wonder's best work. Gliding smoothly, sway-ing easily, he expands one man's financial predicaments into a much wider framework. Get your spirit right, live right and all will come good in the end. He also takes a rare anti-Uncle Sam stance: is it right to send 'kids' off to war for oil? 'Anything is better than the picture of a child/In a cloud of gas.' Co-written by Rosie Gaines, 'Money' was the fifth American single (No 23) and in the UK reached No 11.

Push

A dance groove extolling the virtues of self-motivation and determination. If the track works at all, it is because its energy is every bit as persistent as the lyrics exhort us to be. Ends with raps by Tony M, Prince and Rosie Gaines.

Insatiable

An oozy, squelchy ballad from the Prince manual of seduction ('Scandalous' is the model), it was one of the first songs recorded for the album. His ballad techniques have been so consistent that this might have been written and recorded at any time in the previous 12 years. It was released as a single in the US in November 1991 three weeks before the release of the title track as a single and was

specifically targeted at the R&B market. It made No 3 on that chart, No 77 pop.

Live 4 Love (Last Words From The Cockpit)

Rock from a high place, namely the cockpit of a bomber about to drop its payload. The pilot sets up a pro-peace-and-love, anti-war-and-hate message encapsulating the entire burden of the CD. Be positive, make decisions, take control. Alas, the music is uninspired. The rhythm plods doggedly, the very dull, almost disinterested chorus swathes all else in a cloak of grey, not purple, cloud.

SYMBOL

(FIRST RELEASED OCTOBER, 1992 US PAISLEY PARK/WARNER BROS CD 45037-2, UK VINYL WX 852, CD 9362-45037-2.)

His 14th album, 16 more tracks hot off the presses featuring the New Power Generation and absolutely minimal use of electronic gadgetry, was in the shops a few weeks after the end of the European 'Diamonds And Pearls' tour.

But first, after a year of negotiations, he agreed and signed an extension to his Warner Bros recording contract. Under the old agreement, he was obliged to deliver five more albums. The new deal added one to that number. The extension would give him over time $100m. This figure was broken down as $10m per album for the six more albums, a $20m publishing advance and $20m to restructure the Paisley Park label. His recording royalty would be 25 per cent on every record. He would retain publishing control of Controversy Music but Warners got administrative rights to distribute his original compositions from the catalogue. He would be diversifying into other areas of the media and entertainment fields. He was also appointed a vice-president of Warner Bros Records and given his own office in their Los Angeles headquarters. The company

hoped he would find and attract many new acts to the label.

'We are extremely satisfied with the deal,' Paisley Park Enterprises president Gilbert Davison said. 'It's nice to know that they see him as such a valuable asset.' Previous deals signed by Michael Jackson and Madonna had been worth $60m.

How typical that less than a year after signing this extremely satisfying deal, he should announce his retirement from recording to concentrate on other areas of endeavour. And why not? (A) He had well over 500 unreleased tracks in various stages of preparedness and, (B) he could always change his mind as he did after retiring from live performances in 1985. Indeed, changing his mind would be expected of him. If he didn't change his mind, now *that* would be news.

While working on the next album, Prince

was writing songs for *I'll Do Anything*, a James Brooks film (he directed *Broadcast News* and *Terms Of Endearment*) starring Nick Nolte. But 'Symbol', as it became known, was the main project, again produced, arranged and performed by Prince and the New Power Generation. The personnel had only one change from 'Diamonds And Pearls', Rosie Gaines leaving to work on a solo album for Paisley Park and being replaced by Mayte Garcia, a German-born dancer. Although not officially part of the NPG, Prince had added a DJ, William Graves, to the band for the 'Diamonds And Pearls' tour and a horn section – Brian Gallagher and Kathy Johnson (saxes), Dave Jensen and Steve Strand (trumpets) and Mike Nelson (trombone). They too appeared on the sessions, at Paisley Park, for 'Symbol'.

Prince was by no means the first artist to give an album a symbol as its title. In 1971, the British rock band Led Zeppelin gave just such a 'title' to their fourth album. It was variously referred to as 'Led Zeppelin IV', 'Runes', 'Untitled' and 'Four Symbols', among other names, and caused publishers and typographers numerous headaches. Despite record company resistance to the idea, it went on to become Zeppelin's best selling album ever, perhaps because it contained their epic 'Stairway To Heaven'.

Led Zeppelin's symbology sought to advance their mystic status and suggested dark powers at large. Prince's was more benign and easier to follow. Students of his album sleeves will have plotted the symbol's course through a gradual mingling of the male and female symbols now with an extra curled crossbar added from the symbol used on 'Diamonds And Pearls'. As well as 'Symbol', it is variously known as 'Love Symbol' and 'Androgyny'.

If the use of a symbol as a title was obtuse, the music on the album was less so, although the plot of this 'rock soap opera' telling of the love between a Middle Eastern princess and Prince, was not easily followed. In general, 'Symbol' was 'Diamonds And Pearls Part 2', a patchier collection of tracks spanning the usual pop, rock, funk and ballad formats but here favouring the more upbeat material.

Of the packaging, on the front sleeve Prince, with guitar, plays for and dances with his princess surrounded by her seated hand maidens in the middle of a late 21st century townscape. On the back the tracks, called 'the jams', are printed over a photograph of a pyramid. The tracks are numbered and timed with Roman numerals. Thus track seven which lasts four minutes thirty-eight seconds is: VII Blue Light IV:XXXVIII.

The lyrics are printed small, in white on a dark purple sheet, with a larger script in paler purple sending messages and offering advice. 'may u live 2 see the dawn', 'have u had your 'plus' sign 2 day?', '2 day is the first day of the rest of your life', 'prince's mother's first name is mattie', 'prince likes 2 hug', '2 whomever it may concern, u must come 2 your senses, there are no kings on this earth, only princes', 'prince's favourite food is stewardesses', 'we told u not 2 come 2 the concert', and 'don't buy the black album!' Deciphering was made the more difficult by writing the letters 'e' backwards. Selling the record was made the more difficult, particularly in the USA, by using 'Sexy M.F.' as the first single – a perverse choice making prime-time radio and TV plays almost impossible.

My Name Is Prince

'And I am funky', which is a very assured announcement of self. After falling to earth just south of Cairo to judge by the chorus of eastern harmonies, we're fast into slick, grinding funk. He sings it in a hard, forceful shout, almost screeching some words. This Prince, we learn, was born on the seventh day when God was trying to rest after the small job of creating the Earth and all the other stuff that went with it. He has come for the daughter of the potentate (or whoever) and will 'kick ass' with music to get her. Mixed in is a recapitulation of a favourite theme – money and possessions can't buy salvation. The second half of the track is a rap by co-composer Tony M. The funk loses momentum at this point. 'My Name' was released as the second single off the album and got to No 5 in the UK but only No 36 in the US.

Sexy M.F.

Yes, that was m.f. as in motherfucker. Released as the first single off the album, this is perhaps best seen as Prince's final take on James Brown. He sings it deeper in little more than straight speech. The horns, guitar and syncopated snare drum, the way he calls on the horns section and guitarist Levi Seacer Jr to solo, the song's arrangement are all pure JB while the final Tony M refrain – 'sexy motherfucker shakin' that ass' – is George Clinton taken to the nth degree. How does it progress the storyline? Good point. Prince and his east-ern princess discuss their future in a French Riviera villa, where all the worst soap operas eventually fetch up.

Written with Levi Seacer and Tony M, 'Sexy M.F.' was released before the album as the first single and was not a huge success in the US (No 66) but reached No 5 in the UK.

Love 2 The 9's

A further examination of traditional soul forms. The song is in two parts. The first portion has a hook that is something of a steal from Steely Dan and illustrates how that excellent rock band was influenced by the chord progressions, vocal harmonies and horn arrangements indigenous to black music. This part is sung falsetto.

The second portion of the song is a rap breakdown by Prince and Tony M with a raunchier rhythm and more expansive horn arrangement. The song is clever and complex but has too many 'bits' that do not entirely lock together. Lyrically, '2 The 9's' talks about complete and unequivocal loving to the maximum, much like his early Eighties songs.

The Morning Papers

This guitar-based rock song has a melody and a vocal performance by Prince that might have been written by the very English rock band Squeeze. It explores the nature of young love.

The Max

A hard funk dance track with Tony M getting many of the good lines – 'I wanna shuffle the cards in that stack' – and Michael Bland's loud, muscular drumming dominating.

Blue Light

Prefaced by one of several conversations between Prince and actress Kirstie Alley, who portrays a woman reporter name of Vanessa Bartholomew. He hangs up as soon as she mentions that she's recording the conversations. A rare excursion into reggae and product placement (Evian), 'Blue Light' has a thin melody and a lyric that touches on the small differences that can often make living together all the more difficult. Such as she likes making love in the dark, out of modesty and shyness, he prefers to have a blue light shining. Michael Koppelman plays bass and Eric Leeds adds effective, simple sax.

I Wanna Melt With U

After the rare excursion into reggae, another new departure into techno dance. Not so new is the lyric's sexual slow and slippery, hip-whippin' preoccupations. It does move along the storyline with the Eastern princess: 'Don't look now, but there's a river of blood/U must have been a virgin'.

Sweet Baby

A sweet and gentle mid-tempo soul ballad sung in falsetto bringing comfort to a deserted girl. In the past, he's not often portrayed himself in the role of a comforter unless there's been a piece of the action in the bargain. His motives here are rather more innocent. The song's central theme – stand tall, be proud and brave and better days will come – is of a piece with his post-'Black' thinking. After 'The Max' three consecutive tracks have all been about flow – the undulating reggae of 'Blue Light', the burbling techno of 'I Wanna Melt With U' and now the easy glide of 'Sweet Baby'.

The Continental

Funk and rock and sex spin furiously on the dance floor to very little total effect. Like many of the tracks on 'Symbol', there's a lot of effort expended but the total is considerably less than the sum of its parts. A panting phone conversation with Carmen Elektra brings the track to an abrupt end.

Damn U

A nicely-sung soul slowie in the tradition of 'Do Me Baby'. The song is arranged around piano and strings and takes the 'kooky love affair' of the supposed soap to a stage of satisfactory fulfilment. At the end of the track there's light applause as though we are in an intimate club. 'That was for the lovers,' he says, 'this one is for the whores'. By which, of course, he means the journalists. Re-enter Kirstie Alley in the guise of Vanessa Bartholomew on the quest for answers to some questions. He gives them, putting her on. 'Why are you so arrogant!' she says through gritted teeth.

Arrogance

Is this getting biographical or what? A dislocated, sample-soaked rant segueing via another brief interface with Ms Bartholomew – 'Do you know that the princess is only 16 years old?' she asks – into...

The Flow

On-the-one funk with a rapped vocal by Prince and Tony M who both deeply mistrust hacks and all their works. Strange, since he's manipulated the Press more successfully and for a lot longer without ever having to meet them in any great number. Hereabouts in the soap Prince and his beloved are clearly being hunted down by the vulpine tabloid horde. Instrumentally, the groove is fine and, at the end, there's a good long blow for trombonist Mike Nelson, but what happened to the melodies?

7

One of the better tracks on a bitty album, '7' opens with its chorus chanted a cappella. In a steadily-paced mid-tempo rock song we discover that Prince and his love have become a godly entity steadfast in the knowledge that their enemies – the '7' – will be crushed. Signposted by the mirror-image words – 'Revelation' and 'The Book' – next to the lyrics, the words do indeed correspond to some of the text of the Book of Revelations in the Bible. ('7', of course, is a signifying, symbolical number in many cultures.)

And God Created Woman

Having renamed his keyboard player after one Roger Vadim movie (*Barbarella*), it seems logical that a song should follow. He is Adam, she is his Eve is the news from the soap. The track is a nicely-played mid-tempo soul piece with a lush cushion of trumpets, but again an unmemorable tune.

3 Chains O' Gold

On the generous side, one might see this as a very funny lampoon of Queen at their most pompous, which was very considerable. Certainly, anyone thinking of writing a parody for 'Spinal Tap VIII' will find the job already done. Ludicrously melodramatic and over-wrought, it ends in tears, screams and a horrible death, but not quickly enough.

The Sacrifice of Victor

First, a segue consisting of another attempted interview between Prince and Alley/Bartholomew. The twist being he rings her and condescends to answer some silly questions. Like, his name? Victor not Prince. His age? Three-hundred-and-twenty. Did he know the Crown Princess of Cairo (the girl in the soap) was 16? Was she a member of the NPG? Of course, he is yanking the reporter's chain. But that's easy to do. Shortly after this album was released Prince announced that he was no longer to be addressed by that name. Remarkably, some folks assumed that his new name was Victor because of what he said in the segue. The track ends the album on as funky a note as it came in with some fine blowing from the horn section, good close harmony work by the Steeles and hard driving in the engine room by Michael Bland and Sonny Thompson in the 'Gett Off' groove. The lyric is strongly laced with autobiographical fact, taking as strong an African-American sociopolitical stance as he's ever done.

COME

(FIRST RELEASED 1994 US WARNER BROS CD 45700-2, UK CD 9362-45700-2.)

There is only one thing that is certain in the princedom of P. R. Nelson and that is that nothing is certain. Less than a year after his organisation had expressed extreme satisfaction with the $100m deal signed with Warner Bros in 1992, he was in dispute with the company. In April, 1993, Warner Bros were told that there would be no new studio albums from Prince. Henceforth, he would be delivering packages culled from the capacious Paisley Park vaults which allegedly contained some 500 unreleased tracks. 'After releasing fifteen albums in fifteen years,' a Press release at the time stated, Prince would be 'turning his creative talents to alternative media – including live theatre, interactive media, nightclubs and motion pictures'.

'I just kind of chuckle when I read those things,' his saxophonist Eric Leeds told *Rolling Stone*. 'I say, 'Okay, here he goes again'.' Indeed, there was an unmistakable feeling that we had been in this neighbourhood before. In 1985, towards the end of the Purple Rain tour, he had announced his retirement from live work for a few years. Within months the band was in rehearsal and within 12 months they were on the road again. And so Warner Bros, like Leeds, were sceptical about the veracity of this new announcement. In fact staff reacted to it with considerable jocularity

Readings of the subtext to his recording retirement ranged from his supposed disappointment with the sales of 'Symbol', which were around two million, or a determination to negotiate a change in some area of the contract and deciding that the only way to get what he wanted in a precise area was to bludgeon the whole deal and then retreat until all that was left to debate was his real cause for dissatisfaction.

Eric Leeds's elder brother Alan, who had been Prince's tour manager and later a Paisley Park vice-president, wondered if it were not a wider and more general frustration with the way the music industry released product: record the album, pause, rehearse the stage show, pause, tour, pause, round and round again. This is fine for artists who write and record an album every 18 months to two years, which is roughly the pace of 'mature' acts. But Prince was still writing and recording at the same rate at which he started 15 previously and was frustrated at the inability of the company to just get the music out. So he was keen to release albums under other names, or even no name, and he was keen to use the music in areas other than mere recordings.

But there was a contract to fulfil and so the records had to keep coming, no pun intended. And so not too long after the announcement of his 'retirement', 'Come', a collection of 10 tracks by Prince, was in the shops. Although it is credited as predominantly produced, arranged, composed and performed by Prince, the band and horn section were all involved and David Henry Hwang is listed as co-writer of one cut.

Prince had reportedly begun recording with the word 'SLAVE' emblazoned on his forehead (and George Michael thought he was hard done by) but on this album he is anything but slave material, unless it is to his own passions. Known here as Prince 1958-1993, the

album draws on soul and R&B roots completely ignoring the niceties of pop and, to a very large degree, rock. The lyrics are X-rated with capitals S, E and X but the music is familiar and accessible to anyone familiar with African-American sounds. Of course, the Press has by now ceased to listen to Prince's music, preferring to dwell on the eccentricities of presentation and personality, which are many and far easier to make easy jokes about. A lack of catchy tunes, snappy choruses and gripping hooks did not help widen its appeal.

The 10 songs on the album each have one word titles. The album title 'Come' is indeed as in the climax of the sex act and the sound of waves breaking on a shore, which laps at the start and between each track, is not exactly the most subtle exercise in sexual symbolism you will ever hear. Hollywood and Madison Avenue had used it for decades.

But two of the songs, the title track and 'Letitgo', would stand inclusion on any of the previous 14 albums, most of the grooves are convincing, especially 'Dark', an exceptional lexicon of black music influences, and the subject matter is not a completely unrestricted

diet of sex – cruelty to children and race relations are among the other subjects. Expect this album to be more glowingly reassessed.

The cover shot finds Prince in what looks like a modified page boy suit standing, with walking cane, in front of the impressively Gothic cathedral. It is taken from a book of Terry Gydesen's photographs titled 'Prince presents The Sacrifice Of Victor', a slim and over-priced volume for collectors only. Inside the sleeve, one of the less than cryptic messages reads: 'This is the Dawning of a New Spiritual Revolution'. But the new spirituality was to be achieved by very familiar means.

Come

To the sound of the breaking waves, Prince whispers that if you're over 18, listen up. he got something for you. This is X-rated mid-tempo R&B. The horn section is dead on it for the James Brown band, perhaps more expansive and the bass follows a supple flowing path. By the end of the 10-minute plus track, the arrangement has broadened to become a nineties interpretation of big Marvin Gaye, Isaac Hayes or Barry White productions. The lyrics could not be more explicit. 'Can I suck you baby?/Can I fuck you baby?' A long description of cunnilingus and a longer fade featuring some nice ensemble playing from the NPG horn section, who are fine throughout the CD, is interspersed with what could be the sound of a man eating a pomegranate, a juicy melon or some other succulent fruit. But it's probably meant to be something else.

Space

This track clips along at a sexy, hip-shucking mid-tempo rhythm with a catchy bass line and a cute and decorative keyboard line. Imagine, if you can, a Norman Whitfield rhythm track from 1971/73 with a Temptations vocal arrangement overdubbed by one voice and Smokey Robinson guesting. Endlessly fascinating.

Pheromone

More breaking waves and whispered seduction lead into a snapping 4/4 beat, heavy on the snare drum, above burbling bass. Pheromone, for those who are (a) not zoologists or (b) do not have a dictionary close to hand, is the substance which is secreted and released by animals in order to attract another of the same species. Verily, we are all helpless in the face of a splash of Chanel or Brut, though this may have something to do with choking. The title is sung, catchily, as 'fair moan' and there is a lot of that on the CD too.

Loose!

Uptempo, crazed and chaotic dance rant given some order by the logic of a solid 4/4 drum rhythm. If only the trains ran this regularly. Aside from that, all is looseness with metal guitar riffing and distanced vocals. 'Turn around again,' he sings as though in some

dysfunctional hoedown. Those susceptible to migraine should probably avoid this cut.

Papa

A father on the verge of a nervous breakdown, unable any longer to cope with work or indeed with life itself, is tipped over the edge by his innocent four-year-old child. He locks the kid in the cellar then blows himself away. It is of a piece with the dark and murderous imagery of 'Bob George' from 'The Black Album'. A mid-tempo rock piece, 'Papa' opens as a gentle, if brooding, song and builds inexorably towards a screeching and somewhat discordant showdown.

Race

The waves and whispers this time presage a tight rapped and tighter-arranged polemic about the futility of racial intolerance. 'Race in space are not human/Cut me, cut you both the blood is red,' he singspeaks. 'Face the music' sings sampled Jearlyn Steele Battle as the horn section blares and the crisp rhythm nails down an uptempo beat.

PAGE 112

Dark

A Stax-influenced soul ballad finds Prince, singing in falsetto, deserted by his woman 'and left in the dark'. The horn section colours the first part but the Booker T-like Hammond organ announces Prince's move into one of his rootsiest performances ever, bringing to bear the full artillery of a soul singer's gospel-based vocal effects. It is impossible to believe he had not taken a refresher course from the Specialty label gospel soloists songbook. Exceptional roots music.

Solo

Sung with only the help of a cathedral-like echo and a harp, this self-indulgent experiment forms an interlude not half as haunting as it was meant to be. He's really doomed because 'my name is no one'.

Letitgo

The most commercial track on 'Come' by some distance thanks to the album's catchiest chorus. Taken at a slow walking pace with a tune that slides playfully down the scale, Prince is in the role, again, of someone about to turn their back on a wasteful past life – 'lover here, lover there, who cried, who cared, foolish pride' – and just go with the flow of his feelings. There are numerous 'old' R&B licks and references in here: a funk bass quote, a guitar part transposed to horns, he even briefly scats a solo a la George Benson. Excellent.

Orgasm

A brief climax in most senses of the word. Wailing feedback of a post-Hendrix guitar solo attempt to drown the squeaks, moans and groans of a woman in the throes of sexual pleasure. 'Here I come,' she breathes on the verge of coitus non-interruptus as the waves come pouring out of the speakers. This is not subtle symbolism.

THE BLACK ALBUM

(FIRST RELEASED 1994, SEE BELOW. WARNER BROS US CD 45793-2, UK 9362-45793-2.)

Initially one of the most sought-after and latterly one of the best-selling bootleg albums – estimates start at 200,000 worldwide – 'The Black Album' was finally made generally available through official outlets for a limited period at the end of 1994. (This will not have amused Gord Erickson of Arizona who in 1991 reportedly paid £6,500 for one of only 26 'official' CDs of 'The Black Album' to have been dispatched by Warners.) Copies of the 1994 batch not sold by 31 January, 1995, were to be returned to the distributors.

Bootlegs are predominantly recordings of live concerts. Live radio broadcasts and studio out-takes make up another less substantial portion of the market. But it was, and is, extremely rare for a finished album to be shelved as near to its release date as was 'The Black Album', thus its uniqueness.

What is the fascination of bootlegs? Aside from the thrill of possessing an unauthorised product, they offer a different insight into the workings and ability of the particular artist. A studio album has been laboured over for weeks or months in a studio, its wrinkles ironed out by numerous takes, repeated over-dubs, alteration in the tape speed and so on. These are crafted portraits. By contrast, the live bootleg offers the fan a Polaroid snapshot of the artist. In Prince's case, because he is such a vibrant live performer these snapshots can be interesting, rewarding and big fun.

But 'The Black Album' was even more of a morsel to the bootleg market. Here was an album, much talked about during its recording in the late summer and autumn of 1987 at the end of the European leg of the Sign 'O' The Times tour, which was rumoured to mark yet another change of direction. After the brilliantly expansive music and broad sweep of emotions encompassed by 'Sign', he was said to be returning to the African-American roots of his music – hard R&B-based dance tracks and sexy soul ballads.

At the time it was said that the album had been recorded in an 18 month spell before release. Such a protracted process is completely alien to his usual method. Working in

Minneapolis, he cut four of the eight tracks alone. Two were recorded with the Sign band and two were looted from – or surplus to – other projects. The original plan was for 'The Black Album' to be released on 7 December, 1987. Packaging would be a plain black sleeve – the opposite of The Beatles' 'White Album' – and there would be no advertising or promotion except spins on dance clubs decks. It would to all intents and purposes be the first demo album to get official release in its original state.

So why, a week before released date, did Prince pull the plug on 'The Black Album'? The two main reasons have been cited as pure commercial pragmatism with a little nudge from Warner Bros or a change of heart brought about by personal mental disquiet with the content of the material. Tracks off of 'Sign 'O' The Times' were still selling as singles – 'I Could Never Take The Place Of Your Man' had just been released – and could the market stand another Prince record in the same year that he had released a double set? (Clearly, he had hoped to get round this by leaving his name off the packaging – here is a

disc of music, buy it if you want.)

Other reasons tended to be less plausible – such as he was indignant that the company's pressing plant was giving precedence to other acts, like Madonna, in the weeks before the pre-Christmas bonanza or that the company was shocked by the content of the record. Maybe so, if Warners had somehow failed to take in the lyrics to parts of the 'Dirty Mind' or 'Controversy' or '1999' albums or they had not understood the drift of the then current rap records. Otherwise, I think not.

Another explanation is that 'The Black Album' was indeed a snapshot of his feelings about the contemporary state of the music which used to be his core market and when he'd taken it, he didn't like what he saw. Or heard. Certainly, there is a penchant for images of violence, anger and humiliation, sexual and otherwise, not commonly associated with him. But there is also great energy in the music, an instinctive understanding and feeling for what it is about and how it works, and a loose feel carried over from the extraordinary band jams of the Sign tour.

Bottom line: an announcement from

Prince's kingdom at the time said he made the decision to bail out for personal reasons. Later, he expanded on this saying that he had had a vision during 'a dark night of the soul' which persuaded him that he should can the project. 'I was very angry a lot of the time,' he recalled and he did not want 'that angry, bitter thing to be the last thing' he recorded. His dark night of the soul had given him a strong reminder of the fact that we are mortal and that death can strike us down at any moment. Prince later blamed 'The Black Album' on Spooky Electric, his dark side to the enlightened Camille persona.

Moreover, if business pragmatism had been part of the reason for him pulling the album in 1987, it became in 1994 part of the reason for releasing it. He was in dispute with Warner Bros and wanted to get his contract for six albums over and done with. Albums? He's got 'em in the can and, if he's not touring, he can crank them out at three or four a year. At least.

By the time the album was released in 1994, it sounded, er, seven years old. It had lost a bundle of mystique and was less shocking – or audaciously funny – than, say, 'Head'. The feeling was that there was rather less to 'The Black Album' than met the ear as it veered between the loud and brash and the strangely weak and tinny. Whatever his instincts or motivation for pulling the album in 1987, they were right.

Le Grind

Recorded with the group, 'Le Grind' is a solid dance track driven by a rich bass track and metronomic drumming that develops into a long, structured jam showcasing the band in full steam ahead mode. Mixed into the groove is the complete lexicon of dance party chants and moves – from a few choruses of 'party over here, party over there' to a burst of soul-clapping (i.e. on all eight quaver beats of each 4/4 bar). None of this camouflages the fact that the song has no melody to speak of.

Cindy C

Not much of a tune either to 'Cindy C'. This is again the band having fun on a well-organised, long, straight drive of a funk track. Ms C is a high-class model in France and he spends the song's length trying to get next to her – 'Cindy C, wontcha you play with me, I will pay the usual fee' – with no success.

Dead, On It

Cut alone as a rap lampoon with beat box. He is not impressed with the style. 'See, the rapper first problem stem from bein' tone deaf. Pack the house and try to sing, there won't be anyone left.' Are we feeling threatened? Have we been told we're out of touch with the 'hood? His distillation of the essence of rap is that it consists of lots of gold, cussin' and braggin'. He boasts about a gold tooth that costs more than a house – and an intimate knowledge of women – the sisters like being licked on their knees – and not much more. He would later revise his opinion and have a rapper of his very own.

When 2 R In Love

An earlier, slightly more sparse version of the pretty ballad which appeared on 'Lovesexy', the album which was eventually released as the official follow-up to 'Sign 'O' The Times'. See 'Lovesexy' for fuller discussion.

Bob George

A collision of rap, funk and metal guitar in which Prince comes on like a James Ellroy novel. Seriously psychotic man, short of fuse and long on temper, interrogates his woman about her new coat. He reads it as a present from her man on the side, Bob, who happens to manage Prince, 'that skinny muthafucka with the hiii voice'. Gets mad, shoots her, he comes, cops come, more shots, credits. The speeded up voice of Camille is here replaced by a slowed-down Neanderthal slur (Spooky Electric).

Superfunkycalifragisexy

Mary Poppins meets crazy man Prince on an uptempo dance cut that might have started out as a song for George Clinton (or an homage to him gone wrong). Clinton's one-the-one funk would have been harder, the silly stuff sillier and the sexy stuff more oblique.

2 Nigs United 4 West Compton

A track recorded for the Madhouse album '16', which was being put together in Minneapolis at the same time as 'The Black Album'. Prince, Levi Seacer, Sheila E and Eric Leeds will have been the basic band for the funk-rock-jazz blow-out. Seacer's bass is especially outstanding, first swinging and then funking, like Louis Johnson meets Stanley Clarke.

Rockhard In A Funky Place

A mid-tempo funk cut based on Funkadelic's style and left over from the 1986 Camille sessions. Full of delicious little horn curlicues but as a whole it has an uneven and insubstantial feel because although nothing has been left out, the track simply does not have enough bottom.

THE HITS/THE B SIDES

(FIRST RELEASED SEPTEMBER 1993 US PAISLEY PARK/WARNER BROS CD 45440-2,
UK 9362 45440-2.)

After 14 albums in as many years, Prince eventually released a Greatest Hits collection. Never one to do things by halves, the package contained a generous three CDs with 56 tracks. Four of these songs had not been released before and 20 of the tracks were B-sides of varying obscurity. Moreover, for the occasional fan who did not feel the need to have the complete set of Prince CDs but was satisfied with the Paisley Park selection process, the two 'Hits' CDs could be purchased singly as Volumes 1 and 2.

Although 'The Hits' certainly gave a good impression of the broad sweep of his music over the previous 14 years, there is huge scope for further repackaging of the back catalogue in 'Best Of' and 'themed' issues.

For the purposes of this book, I will review only those new tracks and the B sides, even though some of the 'Hits' appear in versions edited down from the album take.

DISC ONE:

When Doves Cry (see 'Purple Rain'), **Pop Life** (see 'Around The World In A Day'), **Soft And Wet** (see 'For You'), **I Feel For You** (see 'Prince'), **Why You Wanna Treat Me So Bad?** (see 'Prince'), **When You Were Mine** (see 'Dirty Mind'), **Uptown** (see 'Dirty Mind'), **Let's Go Crazy** (see 'Purple Rain'), **1999** (see '1999'), **I Could Never Take The Place Of Your Man** (see 'Sign 'O' The Times'), **Nothing Compares 2 U** (see below), **Adore** (see 'Sign 'O' The Times'), **Pink Cashmere** (see below), **Alphabet St.** (see 'Lovesexy'), **Sign 'O' The Times** (see 'Sign 'O' The Times'), **Thieves In The Temple** (see 'Music From Graffiti Bridge'), **Diamonds And Pearls** (see 'Diamonds And Pearls').

Nothing Compares 2 U

Originally written for The Family, a band formed after The Time stood still. Old Timers Paul Peterson, Jerome Benton and Jellybean Johnson were joined by Miko Weaver,

Susannah Melvoin, Wendy's sister, and Eric Leeds. It was a track off their one and only album ('The Family', Paisley Park, 1985) but never released by them as a single, an omission which Sinead O'Connor opportunely remedied when she covered it in 1988. Had a number one with it, too. This version, a duet between Prince and Rosie Gaines, was recorded live with New Power Generation on the Paisley Park sound stage in January, 1992. The occasion was a post-Superbowl party hosted by Prince after the Washington Redskins stomped the Buffalo Bills at the Minneapolis Metrodome. This version turns the outstanding soul ballad, with its majestic seven-note instrumental refrain, into a heartfelt conversation between separated lovers who need to be reunited but *badly*.

Pink Cashmere

A long, lush falsetto-led ballad finds Prince in utterly-devoted mood. He'll be knitting coats of the said material until his girl comes home again. The track, like the material, is rich and warm. Clare Fischer contributes a soft and fluffy string arrangement. Later in the track, he

improvises like a true soul stepper before winding up into a restrained electric guitar solo on the fade.

DISC TWO:

Controversy (see 'Controversy'), **Dirty Mind** (see 'Dirty Mind'), **I Wanna Be Your Lover** (see 'Prince'), **Head** (see 'Dirty Mind'), **Do Me, Baby** (see 'Controversy'), **Delirious** (see '1999'), **Little Red Corvette** (see '1999'), **I Would Die 4 U** (see 'Purple Rain'), **Raspberry Beret** (see 'Around The World In A Day'), **If I Was Your Girlfriend** (see 'Sign 'O' The Times'), **Kiss** (see 'Parade'), **Peach** (see below), **U Got The Look** (see 'Sign 'O' The Times'), **Sexy M. F.** (see 'Symbol'), **Gett Off** (see 'Diamonds And Pearls'), **Cream** (see 'Diamonds And Pearls'), **Pope** (see below), **Purple Rain** (see 'Purple Rain').

Peach

This 12-bar blues is a straight forward, hard-driving rock 'n' roll hymn to an unattainable good looker. Three rock guitar solos create a mood of increasing desperation.

Pope

'You don't understand,' rages 'Pope' Bernie Mac, a Def Jam comedian, 'I ain't scared a youmuthafucka'. With a co-lead by Mayte Garcia, Prince's boombasscious rap is wrapped around a pretty chorus of 'You can be the President, I'd rather be The Pope'. The President, you see, gets his legislation snagged in Congress or the Senate. No power. The Pope don't have such problems. Not one for Catholics. Or politicians for that matter.

DISC THREE

Hello

The B-side of 1985's 'Pop Life' in the US, and of 'Raspberry Beret' in the UK, 'Hello' is a driving up-tempo dancer performed with The Revolution and using a 'typical' Prince organ riff. The lyric is not typical, being one of the few occasions when he used his music as a forum for a very specific comment about what was happening in his life. He had not wanted to sing on the 'We Are The World' track in aid of famine relief but had offered a song ('4 The Tears In Your Eyes') to the US for Africa pro

ject and everyone was happy until the Press started pestering him and questioning his commitment and motives. 'Hello' was an answer. There is just as much hunger among the under-privileged at home in the USA, he sings, and he's more than happy with his record on benefits and charity work. Interesting simply because he chose, for once, to address an issue immediately and without obliqueness.

200 Balloons

The flip of his fourth No 1, 'Batdance', '200 Balloons' is a harder rock out-take from the 'Batman' soundtrack and a more frantic continuation of the 'Batdance' party mood. A myriad sampled snatches from the film and elsewhere are splattered throughout the track.

Escape

The 'Lovesexy' track 'Glam Slam' was so unsuccessful as a single that it isn't on 'The Hits' but this was its B-side. 'Escape', a clarion call to get on the dance floor, re-treads the chorus and other portions of the A-side.

Gotta Stop (Messin' About)

The first non-album track issued on a single. When 'Let's Work' off 'Controversy' was first released as a 7" single 'Ronnie Talk To Russia' was on the flip. However, for the 12" dance re-mix released in the USA in February, 1982, 'Gotta Stop' replaced it. An out-take from the 'Dirty Mind' sessions, it's a typical Prince stomp of the time, sung in falsetto with squeaky organ, the track was released as the A-side of a 7" single. Twice. In the space of two 1982 months. In June it had 'Uptown' on the B-side, in July 'I Wanna Be Your Lover' was its flip. Yep, the record company really knew what it was doing.

Horny Toad

B-side to the 1983 US pop Top 10 hit 'Delirious' off '1999', 'Horny Toad' is a 12-bar organ-dominated rock 'n' roller. In the UK it was the B-side of 'Little Red Corvette'.

Feel U Up

First recorded around 1982/3, 'Feel U Up' eventually emerged in a 1989 rearrangement as the B-side to 'Partyman', the 'Batman'

track. It appeared in (Short Stroke) and (Long Stroke) versions for 7" and 12" release. This is the shorter take. It is a Groper's Charter.

Girl

The flip of the 1985 single 'America' (US) and 'Pop Life' (UK) from 'Around The World In A Day'. Performed with The Revolution. Many of the B-sides have interesting ideas about either arrangement or instrumentation and here the rhythm is carried by a steady keyboard throb and fingerpops. The lyric is less unexpected – hot desire and seduction turning bodies into a 'sea of electricity'. 'If I was anything else, I'd be the water in your bath,' he sings.

I Love U In Me

The word is 'aching'. Used as the B-side of 'The Arms of Orion' (1989) from 'Batman' and 'Insatiable' (1991), the 'Diamonds And Pearls' track, this is an outstanding ballad. Its excel-lent, layered vocal arrangement delivers the sort of testimonial to a girlfriend's sexual prowess that gets Cabinet ministers sacked. But it's tenderly, exquisitely done and the woman here is in charge. One can't quite

imagine anyone else having the courage to sing it.

Erotic City

One of his more celebrated B-sides, 'Erotic City' was recorded with The Revolution and turned up on the flip of his second US No 1, 'Let's Go Crazy' (1984). A jaunty pop-funk out-take from the 'Purple Rain' sessions, it got considerable airplay in the States. In the UK, it appeared on the 12" of 'Let's Go Crazy' and was also used later on other 12" singles.

Shockadelia

An out-take from the Camille sessions, this unexceptional mix of rock, funk and silly voices was assumed to be a mild dig at Jesse Johnson, the original guitarist with The Time, who after he had jumped ship, called his debut album 'Shockadelica' but omitted to include a song of that name on it. Or was he lampooning Michael Jackson's 'Thriller'? 'If I Was Your Girlfriend' was the top-side.

Irresistible Bitch

An out-take from the '1999' sessions, the fast-moving cut became the B-side of 'Let's Pretend We're Married' (1983) when backing vocals by Wendy Melvoin and Lisa Coleman were added. It came out only in the US – in the UK B-sides at this time tended to be other album tracks in an attempt to get his LP sales moving.

Scarlet Pussy

Another out-take from the Camille sessions, 'Scarlet Pussy' was the B-side to 'I Wish U Heaven' a 1988 flop off 'Lovesexy'. Sheila E is a featured singer and Prince's voice, slowed down, narrates the story of this alley cat. The skittish funk track and the lyric's mix of cartoon humour and sexual imagery will be familiar to students of the George Clinton catalogue.

La, La, La, He, He, Hee

According to Alan Leeds, annotator of the 'Hits/B Sides' collection, Prince was challenged to make a song out of this unpromising

title. He co-wrote it with Sheena Easton. They took the images of cats and dogs from the previous track and, with canine howls and yelps, fashioned an increasingly catchy, funky and very silly pop song. It was the B-side of 'Sign 'O' The Times' (1987).

She's Always In My Hair

The flip to 'Raspberry Beret' (US) and 'Paisley Park' (UK) in 1985 found Prince and The Revolution knee-deep in Beatles pop hooks. The track had a tight little guitar solo and re-emerged as an addition to the stage shows of 1993.

17 Days

One of the very best B sides, '17 Days' was on the flip of 'When Doves Cry'. Melodically and in certain aspects of arrangement it bears very close resemblance to another Minneapolis production – Jimmy Jam and Terry Lewis's ballad 'A Broken Heart Can Mend' which was cut by Alexander O'Neal. Prince's song is pacier.

How Come U Don't Call Me Anymore

Sung with only acoustic piano and multi-tracked vocal harmonies for company, this was a live favourite back in the days when he played a segment of the set seated at the 88s. It was used as the B-side to '1999', his first UK Top 30 entry.

Another Lonely Christmas

A conversation with a dead, dearly departed love, this was the B-side of, aptly enough, 'I Would Die 4 U'. Recorded with The Revolution, it has the same echoing vocals used on other tracks laid down for 'Purple Rain'. In fact, it has the title track's rather grand sweep without quite matching its anthemic chorus. Bearing in mind his reputation for rising to challenges, it might be someone dared him to mix two rock genres – the Christmas song and the Death song – in one?

God

The B-side of 'Purple Rain' sounds like a typically left-field attempt at re-fashioning gospel music in the late 80s. His unsettling squeaks and squeals, which come at the beginning and end of the track, are not unlike those heard in the work of many of the great gospel tenors when they sail off into falsetto. Gospel handclaps, too, point to the sanctified seriousness of the recording. The meat of the lyric is a distillation of parts of the Book of Genesis. A weird take on gospel though, you won't hear this in the Amen Corner at too many churches.

4 The Tears In Your Eyes

Originally recorded for the 'We Are the World' famine relief album, this is a previously unreleased version recorded at Paisley Park by Prince with Wendy Melvoin and Lisa Coleman.

Power Fantastic

A final, previously unreleased track with The Revolution. 'Power Fantastic' was scheduled for The Dream Factory project and recorded at the then very newly opened Paisley Park complex. It found Prince at the dawning of a new era of experimentation with horns. The colours added by Eric Leeds's flute and Atlanta Bliss's muted trumpet, often credited to Miles Davison bootlegs, are central to the arrangement. And, praise be, the piece took a rare step outside 4/4 time. It is regrettable that Prince has not ploughed this furrow more often.

A truly great example of the pop song as prayer, the contrast between desperate verse and achingly beautiful chorus is poignant and heart-stopping.

BIBLIOGRAPHY

Prince: Inside The Purple Reign, Jon Bream (Collier/Macmillan, 1984)

Prince, Steven Ivory (Bantam, 1985)

Prince: Imp of the Perverse (Virgin, 1988)

Prince: A Pop Life, Dave Hill (Faber & Faber, 1989)

Prince: An Illustrated Biography, John W. Duffy (Omnibus, 1992)

Prince: A Documentary, Per Nilsen (Omnibus, 1993)

INDEX

Printed in Great Britain by Printwise (Haverhill) Limited, Haverhill, Suffolk 7/99 (34795)